Chestnut Review

VOLUME 1
2019–2020

Second Edition

Chestnut Review
Ithaca, New York
https://chestnutreview.com
Chestnut Review appears four times a year online, in January, April, July, and October, and once per year in print in July.

ISSN 2688-0350 (online)
ISSN 2688-0342 (print)
ISBN 978-1-965158-00-5

Chestnut Review

CONTENTS

Year One in Review

Looking back, 2019 seems so far away. For most of us, "pre-pandemic" feels like a fairy tale. Nostalgia tends to the rose-colored, of course, but pre-COVID feels even more so. Little did we know that the rumblings of a new virus would subsequently change almost everything about the way we live.

In the spring of 2019, our little group of co-conspirators decided that it was time: the preparation work was done, we'd made spreadsheet after spreadsheet that had said yes, this project could work, and all that remained was to line up everything and pull the trigger. We had our Submittable account, we'd made the webpage, we'd set the submission guidelines, and we'd listed on Duotrope. Any further delay would be simply to satisfy nerves, to put off the terrifying moment for any small business when you open the doors, literally or figuratively, and...wait. Wait to see if anyone is interested in what you offer. Wait to see if that transmits into more than a single visitor or sale. Wait to see if trends begin that suggest you will be able to continue, or if you are going to be a flash in the pan that quickly subsides.

Just as it's difficult to remember life pre-pandemic, it's hard to recall exactly what we felt as we started this magazine. We have notes, of course, sometimes absurd scrawls of plans and adjustments that needed to be made, but mostly what we can't remember is how it felt. But based on our experiences over the subsequent five plus years, there must have been stress, anxiety, worry, just as there was elation and excitement as submissions came in, as we saw how strong they were, and how yes, we could make a magazine that presented work that we were proud to present to the world, responded quickly, and paid its artists.

We forever will be eternally grateful to those who submitted to us starting that May and throughout our first year, as well as to those who accepted our offer and appear in these pages. They took our promises seriously, having nothing to base them on but faith—we had no previous issues, no track record of running an international magazine, no real reason that we should succeed—yet they bet on us. And so, they will always be dear to us as part of our inaugural issue. Quite frankly, they created us.

Year One Statistics

5/15/2019-5/14/2020

Submissions received:
4,843

Pieces published:
48
(12 art, 28 poetry, 8 prose)

Acceptance rate:
.9911%

Chestnut Review

Volume 1 Number 1 Summer 2019

FOR STUBBORN ARTISTS

CONTENTS

Cover: Claire Elliott, "Pink Varietals"
24" x 30", Oil on Canvas, 2018

Introduction

Welcome to our unexpected beginning. I say "unexpected" because, of course, this was supposed to be the Autumn issue. But fate had better things for us in store. As we reviewed over a thousand submissions, it became patently clear that we wanted an interim issue, a place to hold these amazing works, because we could not possibly fit them into what we planned for October. A typical problem when you are faced with reams of good, solid literature and art, but one that is emotionally difficult to deal with. And so we struggled, trying to fit it all into one issue, to make hard decisions, before we realized that we simply didn't want to. So we broke our own rules. This can't happen again, of course, because otherwise we'd be publishing every month, but this once we can pull it off. And so, here is the Summer issue, our first ever.

We kept to our principles: though we were completely prepared to refund submission fees for work which was considered for longer than a month, we stayed on task and made decisions within that window for each and every one. That, to us, means something. That we have committed to this model and mean to see it through. While the vast majority of those submissions had to be rejected, and rejections are never fun to receive or to send, we consider it our responsibility to inform you as quickly as we can so that you can send out your next batch. I hope you feel we met that goal. By the way, for those of you who like to know these things, six of our artists this month submitted work during our free submission period, proof positive that you don't have to pay a fee to have your work selected.

On to the richness: **Alana Benson** describes meeting a singular young man in "Jared." **Laura Johnson's** "in the garden" envisions the kind of growing many of us are guilty of. **Deb Nordlie** captures the trials and tribulations of young love in "David Dunston once threw a rock at my head." **Eric Roller** vividly depicts the breaking of a family in "The Vacation." **Carl Boon** describes a moment between fear and revelation in "Rivermonsters." **Annie Stenzel** brings heartbreaking emotion to "On learning of the suicide of an 11-year old boy I didn't know." **Robert L. Penick** hits on parts of life that aren't lost with age in his "Things We Don't Get Over." **Brendan Connolly** had us in stitches with his "#20" sketch, and **Laura Gill** lyrically examines sisterhood in "Mary and Martha." Our cover art, "Pink Varietals," is by **Claire Elliott**, and we are pleased to feature the painting "Corner of the Hemingway House" by **Timothy F. Phillips** and the lovely photograph "Springtide" of **Nam Nguyen**.

We're grateful to these artists for taking a chance on us, considering that before May, we didn't exist. We hope you'll spend time with all of these pieces, and appreciate them as much as we did.

Until autumn, then. Keep creating, and being stubborn about it all.

James Rawlings

David Dunston once threw a rock at my head

David Dunston once threw a rock at my head.

Everyone was gone when his snowballs
began to pelt my window
and from my gate, I heard his love call,
"Debbie is a Pickle-Head. Debbie is a Pickle-Head."
That's when I knew he loved me.

Before going outside to throw a snowball at him,
because, you see, I loved him too,
I changed my shirt, then my pants.
I brushed out my hair and polished it into a neater ponytail,
even adding a red ribbon left over from Christmas.
Not satisfied with the arrangement or sheen of my tresses,
I started again, the ribbon left on the floor—it had to be just right.
My darling was outside.
Waiting.
A dab of Mom's Chanel #5 would cinch the deal,
so I touched its cold glass stopper
to my wrists and throat.
Then I was ready to be Juliet to his Romeo.
Oh, visions of our future life were clear to me:

all the kids at school would finally know how much I was adored.
He'd hold my hand at recess.
We'd live in his father's motel,
moving from room to room at will,
and eat only at his father's restaurant.
I would never again be bothered with dishes.
He was irresistible.

In my winter coat,
I raced to the front door and opened it,
propelled by his siren's song.
With the joy that comes
from greeting one's own true sweetheart,
I leaned over to gather the most perfect white snow to lob
        at my beloved—
because then he'd know how much I adored him.
But Cupid's snowy arrow
clobbered me first: hard and sharp,
for inside his rounded cannonball of affection
was a jagged grey rock, hidden, unlike his love for me.

It pierced my head on the left side—
the same side as my heart—
but my devotion for him
was more potent than my pain.

My blood splattered into frosty pools
gaudy on the snow,
my red dripping onto the white field of winter.
The drops rained
and created my own personal Rorschach test,
its pattern open to his ten-year-old interpretation.

There by my front steps
was exposed my garnet bouquet of love on the glittering ice.
For him.
For him.
He laughed. "Debbie is a Pickle-Head. Debbie is a Pickle-Head."
I had never known such worship.

I tell you all this because Nancy, my sister-in-law,
wanted to know why my hair is always flat on the left side.
"Oh," I answered, "it's because David Dunston once loved me."

The Vacation

In Gettysburg, PA
we stand on a pond bank
pretending to watch
the walleye
nip at the stranded damselflies

Mom picks up a rock
throws it into the water and
says what I already know,
what I have known for a long time:
I can't take this anymore.

"Not here," Dad says,
and before the rings melt
back into the water,
pushes me from the scene:
"Go play."

I stumble over the pond's
sandy berm and loll
toward a brass horse
rearing on its haunches
beneath a sycamore.
The Union cavalryman bayonets

holes into the humid air
with a metallic fury on his lips.
His Confederate enemy
hides in a bed of ivy
reaching out in surrender.
We sit together
the three of us
pleading,
our scenes
unfolding and
eventually settling.
Treaties are made,
pacts established,
and then a customary resignation
seats itself
amongst the monuments.
I am ready to broker
the compromise.

Back at the truck
Dad anticipates my question:
"She's taking a little vacation," he says
waving at the road behind us.
I turn and see her
walking,
her right arm balancing
a leather suitcase
bouncing tightly
against her left hip

#20

at a bar in brooklyn late at night, a woman taps me on the shoulder and asks if she heard me correctly, that i/d seen hamilton twice?

i had made a joke to jackie the woman overheard and apparently she took it very seriously

well, i say, only once really. the second time tom brought giselle and the kids, but they started crying and we had to leave early

excuse me, she says, tom and giselle?

yeah, i say sipping my beer casually, my cousin tom. you might know him, tom brady?

on the subway back to her apartment, jackie leans her head against my shoulder and i can see her reflection in the glass across the car

you know, she says closing her eyes, in the whole time i/ve lived here, i dont think i/ve ever seen someone so likely to be stabbed for a good reason

CARL BOON

Rivermonsters

Dean Jones had a theory.
Dean Jones had acne on his shoulders
and was tall, so we believed him
when he said that there were monsters
in the river and more—
ghosts of hobos in the old plantation house
off State Route 38, the Old Savannah Highway.
Being a storybook boy, I believed
they were the same, dead slaves
who'd returned to draw catfish out of slumber
then frolic where their masters had.
So it rained for a week, the remnants
of the Sea Islands hurricane,
and Dean Jones said when the sun comes back
we'll go down to the Bottoms
in boots and see. They put me in charge
of the sabers and sandwiches, his brother Len
the map, and Sadie Tomlinson the spells
because she never smiled and her mother
was a witch. Expecting busted shackles
and bits of Sherman's clothes, perhaps a whip
or a gourd that rattled, I went in first.
What amazed me were the ladybugs,
shields of them everywhere like poppies

in the spring, black and red, and when
I told them it was beautiful, when I told them
it was like a dream, they wouldn't believe me.
Perhaps the hurricane made them;
perhaps some unnamed mother
brought them forth to remind us
there was some joy we'd missed, some power
that even the United States of America
failed to conjure with their real bayonets
and dark blue jackets. Another century
was coming, and among our ham salad sandwiches
that afternoon we believed—even Dean Jones
believed—that it would be better than the last.

Right: Nam Nguyen, "Springtide." Photograph of cacti garden,
Honolulu, Hawaii, April 2001.

On learning of the suicide of an 11-year-old boy I didn't know

The first response is incredulity: eyes wide
in hope of having misread the message. Salt
scratch-leaps to make tears; throat catches because
breath won't pass through paralysis. Pity
and sympathy hand in hand with horror.

By the time true compassion comes, I can't
un-know how altered that poor family's
life will be, split into before and after, never
resuming its former course, each year the landmark
anniversary with its mountain of wreckage.

Into the echoes that separate me from true grief,
my hands lift to wring and plead. I want to shriek
at the phantom youth: oh, child! you have murdered
the wrong person. The boy you killed was only
a stranger passing through whoever you were going to be.

L A U R A   G I L L

Mary and Martha

"Preachers or scientists may generalise, but we know that no generality is possible about those whom we love"

E.M. Forster, Howard's End

I grew up going to church, but I never learned the story of Mary and Martha. More specifically, I never knew there was a Martha at all. I knew there was a Mary, but I never knew she had a sister Jesus didn't like. In the story, Jesus visits their house and Mary walks over to Jesus and sits at his feet. Martha continues to cook and clean. When Martha asks for her sister's help, Jesus tells her: "you are worried and upset about many things, but only one thing is needed. Mary has chosen what is better, and it will not be taken away from her."

Say "Martha." Martha forces your tongue between your teeth. You need to get the air just right, too—it requires a minor strain. To say Mary, you only move your lips; your mouth need not deal with the muscle trapped inside it.

Growing up, I did know that I had two older sisters and a younger brother. They were bodies with flesh and bone. And yet, they were also constructions of my own making—people connected to me whose formation formed my own. One of my sisters was eighteen years ahead of me, and so it was my immediate older sister whose construction I had at the ready—an older sister is not just an older sister but a person to follow, to see which parts of oneself measure up or don't. Growing up, I wanted to be my sister because she was older. And I wanted to be my sister because she had blonde hair and light eyes and an athletic body. I had dark hair, a stomach I could never "suck in," and a bottom lip my sister often told me was "too big."

My sister was not just good at sports, she was good at performing in school plays, and both things brought her confidence. I wanted confidence. I didn't know how to get it without her build and her looks. I only knew how to be overwhelmed by what I did not know. I remember being in sixth grade, and not being able to stay in the room when the class had to dissect a frog. I did not know how anyone could move their tiny hearts to see what was below. I often found my head separated from the rest of my body; at a dance or on a sports field, I'd feel like I was floating above the crowd. I hated reading out loud, and would often mumble—not because I didn't know the words but because I wanted to get to each one too quickly, without knowing exactly what they meant.

In Joan Didion's essay about Georgia O'Keefe, the essay closes with an image of O'keefe and her sister, Claudia, walking into the Texas sunset, "away from town and toward the horizon." As they walk, her sister throws bottles into the air and then shoots them. Didion is right when she says "in a way one's interest is compelled as much by the sister Claudia with the gun as by the painter Georgia" because it's true—I can't stop thinking about Claudia. I watch her throw her bottles into the air, and I imagine them shattering. I see the glass shards flying in the big pink and orange sky.

It's too easy to say that all sisters are Martha and Mary, and it's too simple to say that Martha had no Mary and Mary had no Martha. And yet: I wonder if every woman, sister or not, has to at least reckon with Mary and Martha because they do seem to be everywhere within me: Martha tells me to clean the house when guests come. Mary tells me to let it be. Then, they wrestle, and distract me with their intertwined legs, as they pull at one another's hair. I wonder which one is hurting me.

Martha:
Hebrew meaning: bitter.
American meaning: bitter.
Aramaic meaning: lady.
Biblical meaning: one who becomes bitter; provoking.
How, then, to become a lady?

Before I knew about Mary and Martha, I thought of my two grandmothers as Mary and Martha, even though I didn't yet know roots of those archetypes. My father's mother was the Mary, and my mother's mother, the Martha. My father's mother would dote on us, and smother us with kisses. She always seemed impressed with our accomplishments, trivial as they were, and we called her Granmére because she loved to sing French lullabies to us as we fell asleep. My mother's mother was called Nonnie, and even though that name is derived from the Italian, Nonna, she was not Italian, nor particularly interested in Italy. She hated garlic, and was interested in using one's hands as much as possible—to sew, to knit, to cook, to change sheets, to pick the towels up from the floor.

And yet, there were crossovers. For one thing, they both married people they weren't "supposed" to; Granmére, a Presbyterian, married a Catholic before graduating from college, and Nonnie, a twenty-eight-year-old nanny, married her employer's older brother, sixteen years her senior. And so, looking back, I can see that it wasn't so simple after all. One time, Nonnie danced to the trumpet in a barn in Switzerland; Granmére raised seven children.

Susan Fenimore Cooper was an environmentalist and a writer during the 1800's when there weren't many women who were environmentalists and writers, and she wrote about what she saw in nature as a way to justify women's subordination. When it came to sap trees, she saw them give and give and give, and remain "perfectly healthy," saying "one would think that the loss of so much sap would necessarily injure the trees; but it is not so, they remain perfectly healthy, after yielding every spring, gallons of the fluid."

In some ways, Susan Fenimore Cooper was right: the sap does arrive again, the trees are able to give year after year. At the start of spring, sugary water drips out of their centers, and into cans, making a pinging sound as its droplets hit the bottom.

But I wonder: what did she make of the tapping—the sharp object needed to puncture the bark, to rip at the skin? Does every tree recover?

My friend is a teacher and he says that when he sees girls being mean to one another, he gives them the same speech. He tells them that their fighting is what "the man" wants. He tells them about the pervasive patriarchy. He warns them against fighting one another because then they will have not have each other as allies. He tells them that their bitterness will keep them down.

No one wants a bitter woman at all.

What Mary's name gets that Martha doesn't is the "sea"—it means "sea of bitterness, sea of sorrow." Some say, it means a "drop of the sea," a "star of the sea," "the wished-for-child," the "mistress of the sea." Her bitterness is washed away in the sea; her sorrow is full of deep blues and greens. There are creatures within her that live and breathe underwater, full of feeling.

"How'd she do it?" People often ask, when they talk about Granmére, and her seven children— "How'd she manage to do it all, and with such grace?" Grace seems to be code for beauty or something like beauty—the kind you can only achieve if, along with a small frame and high cheekbones, you can also smile, laugh, and be generous with others. "How'd she do it?"

No one wonders how Nonnie did it. No one wonders how she "did it" because, in a way, she didn't "do it." Yes, she raised her children, took care of the members of the town, cooked, travelled, cleaned, read the newspaper, and went to church every Sunday, but she did not "do it" because she wore her grievances on her sleeve, and she did not hide her discontent. She was also slightly overweight, and never seemed to care.

Nonnie wanted all her granddaughters to become teachers. My sister became an actress and comedian, and I became a teacher. I invested all my creative energy into lesson plans, class activities, and feedback forms. I decided the part of myself that enjoyed writing was the same part of myself that enjoyed teaching, and so I stopped writing. I was a practical woman, with a practical life, and practical work. I was not frivolous. I was fraught.

In Vermeer's "Christ in the House of Martha and Mary," Mary sits at the foreground, in a blue-grey skirt and red, long-sleeved shirt. Her feet are exposed, and her legs cover Jesus's shins. Jesus's legs are spread, and he is tilting back. A royal blue blanket covers his lap, and part of his left shoulder. His right hand points toward Mary, as his face turns toward Martha, who stands behind him, setting down a basket of bread, her face turned away from the light. If you didn't know the story of Mary and Martha, it would look like an image of two women waiting on Jesus, ready and glad to meet his every need. He looks so satisfied, as if he's just won a match. If you know the story, you know that part of what is bringing Jesus satisfaction is actually what he is saying to Martha as he points to Mary, saying: "this, this Martha, this is the right way to be." And yet: the bread looks so warm and sturdy, and Martha's white sleeves are radiant. Even just to look at the placement of Jesus's body, the way it is almost split in half between the two women, tells a different version of the story. Both are needed. Both are good. At least in the eyes of a man. He has a wife and a mistress.

When my sister got her first boyfriend, I wrote him a letter, telling him to stay away. I wanted to be like my sister, but I also wanted her attention—I didn't appreciate his infiltration, and how he took her from me. It made me sick to watch her flirt with him, and even more uncomfortable to see how she enjoyed it. I wrote it in a fury. They were sitting in her room, chatting, and I was sitting in mine, crying and writing. I couldn't figure out if I was jealous of him or of her and, of course, it was both. I never gave him the letter, and I never showed it to my sister. I tucked it away in a notebook in my desk.

A family friend asked, "How are you doing?" and I said, "Good." "Then your sister," she said with a look of concern, "cannot be doing well." She was a social worker, and she said, in her experience, "sisters are always cancelling one another out. Both are rarely happy at the same time."

Some sap trees take longer to recover than others.

In *Howard's End*, the sisters, Margaret and Helen, are rarely happy at the same time. The book starts with Helen announcing a hasty engagement, and Margaret's attempts to be sympathetic through worry and concern. She sends her aunt to suss out the situation, and by the time her aunt gets there, the engagement is off. Margaret is relieved, and Helen, too, for a time. After Helen returns, they host dinner parties full of heated conversations about the suffrage movement, inequality, and politics, and then, Margaret decides to marry Henry—the older, richer neighbor, who embodies all of the stereotypes of the old guard, with his stodgy, stuck-up ways. The sisters become estranged; they don't seem to understand one another anymore. In the film version, Helen receives a letter from Margaret, and says: "This isn't Margaret." A few scenes later, Margaret receives a postcard from Helen and says, "The postcards don't seem to have come from her, that's not her." It's as if the sisters believe they know one another better than they know themselves.

When Jesus came over, did Martha look at Mary, and think, "Oh stop it, that's not you." Did Mary look at Martha and wonder, "Why this show? Just relax a little bit." Or did they let it go, knowingly understanding their roles, and who one another might play.

In the film version of *Howard's End*, Margaret is played by Emma Thompson, and Helen is played by Helena Bonham Carter. A few years after making the movie, Emma Thompson's husband, Kenneth Branagh, left Emma Thompson for Helena Bonham Carter, and I know they are playing sisters in the film, I know they are not really sisters, and yet, it feels like a different kind of betrayal when you know they acted as sisters, and that they played those sisters in particular.

Martha doesn't want to be Mary. Even after Jesus tells her that Mary's way is right, Martha does not change. She doesn't become doting and docile. In fact, she challenges him, after her brother, Lazarus, dies and Jesus arrives to help. She steps out of the house and says, "if you had been here, my brother would not have died." It isn't that she doesn't believe in Jesus, or doubts he will be able to perform a miracle, it's simply that she's angry, and she needs him to know. Even when he goes to resurrect the body, she cannot hide her frustration—she says, "but Lord, by this time there is a bad odor, for he has been there four days." It's the kind of thing you say when you want to say something else— "well, now the food is cold," you say, even though you know you can warm it up again, even though you know what you want to say is: "I'm annoyed you've come to dinner so late."

On my recent birthday, my father told me, "you saved the family." On each birthday, he has said something similar: "you really made us want to have another," "you were just such a bright light, a real joy." There is a part of me that feels badly for my sister when I hear that, and another part of me that is proud I was such a "joy." My sister, who came two and a half years before me, was not a "happy baby." She is often described as a "grumpy baby" and a "stubborn baby" and a baby who took the energy out of my mother. Her first word was "more." My first words were "ball" and "duck," and I was often happy to sit in a chair and observe the world around me.

Susan Fenimore Cooper used the environment to justify her feelings that women had a natural place in the world. As such, she didn't believe in women's suffrage. She wrote, in her "Letter to the Christian Women of America," that the natural position of woman is clearly, to a limited degree, a subordinate one." She believed this because she believed that both physically and intellectually women were weaker than men. Beyond the physical and intellectual, she thought it was a religious duty to maintain the subordinate role. She wrote that Christianity "protects her far more effectually than any other system," and that "precious rewards are promised to every faithful discharge of duty, even the most humble." And yet, Jesus scolded Martha. She was not "rewarded" for feeding her family. Nor was she protected. She was told her subordination wasn't right—it wasn't exactly what was being called for. He wanted: a little less demanding, a little more humble, just a little more fawning.

Just a little more sap. Give from the tap a little more.

The worst thing one Mary did was to bring her pet lamb to school, and of course she wasn't punished, really—the lamb simply had to wait ("patiently, patiently") for her to return. The song tells us the lamb was the diversion only a Mary could create: an innocent, lighthearted one. The kind that no one really gets mad about, but simply shakes their head while holding back a smile. Oh Mary, you're so silly—oh little lamb, you're so sweet, your fleece is white as snow.

There aren't any children's songs about Martha.

My family makes maple syrup, and the time for collecting sap can be as short as two days or as long as three weeks, and when we were kids, we felt lucky if we could join the men on the truck. It only happened once or twice, but I remember being encouraged to put my mouth under the spigot and drink the cold, sweet water. It was better than the syrup, I thought, better than the gooey, thick, warm liquid they put into tiny plastic cups for sampling. I wanted to stay there, with my head turned toward the tree and my shoulder pressing into the bark; I wanted to stay and taste the source.

What I didn't know then is that there are other species of maple trees that make sap, and there are other textures of sap, in other trees, too. And recently, scientists discovered something new about maple trees—it turns out saplings can produce as much sap as mature trees. It turns out age makes no difference. What came before is as good as what comes after—it's the same stuff.

I got engaged before my sister, and a few people told me they were so pleased I did. They said it in a tongue-and-cheek way, with a nudge and a wink, but I always felt strange when they said that, not just because I knew my sister wanted to be engaged to her partner, but because I had no control in the matter. I did not choose when this would happen. And she, too, felt as if, in some ways, she had no control. She got engaged soon after, and our weddings were months apart. We got married in different countries, but we both wore short dresses, and refused to have sit-down dinners. Both weddings ended in a circle, with flowing beer, and a singalong.

Martha could not replace Mary, nor could Mary replace Martha. Both are needed, and yet: we know about Mary, and we do not know as much about Martha. We seem incapable of being able to see both, or to keep both in our collective narrative. Is that because Jesus was right, or is it because we are desperate for order and order looks like rungs on the ladder, one above the other? Perhaps it's not just a need for order, but an assumption of order, or a decision to be ordered.

The more I wonder about Martha, the less I feel that she was robbed of something. I feel simply that she was denied something, which is not to say she needed Jesus's praise, but that she could have used it, or at least a different form of it. What I mean by that is: what would it have looked like if Nonnie's type of beauty was acknowledged, as much as her knitting, cooking, and demanding nature was? What if Granmere was praised for her recklessness at times, as well as what appeared to be her calm, cool demeanor in the face of chaos? What if I wasn't just a "happy baby," but an oblivious one; what if my sister wasn't just a demanding baby, but one who knew her needs and asserted them? Most of us know there's much more to each of us than appears in the narratives we tell, so why do I care?

I care because there are many ways to praise, and so rarely do we embrace the multitude. I care because it's rare to be in a women's restroom without hearing the word, "sorry." I'm sorry for opening the door too fast, for being in the way of the mirror when you need to check your eyebrows. I'm sorry for caring about my eyebrows more than my clean hands. I'm sorry for cleaning my hands too long. I care because I am sorry for being scared; I'm sorry for not being more bold. I care because my aunt was sorry when she wrote in her journal about a huge blizzard in 1888, and though her account is full of glorious details, she apologizes for writing about it at all. She writes: "there must have been great suffering...I can't remember anything only as it affected me & family," and then she signed it, "Selfish Aunt Emma."

I'm not sure a woman could have written *Howard's End*, and by that I mean—perhaps a woman could have written *Howard's End*, but I would venture to guess it would end differently. In the book, the sisters choose one another over their other lives. Margaret does stay in her marriage, but only because her husband has a change of heart about Helen, only because he grows to accept her sister into their life. The film ends with a shot of Helen in the field, with her baby attached to her chest. She looks happy, and we are meant to believe that happiness is connected with Margaret's. It's true that many sisters choose one another, but it's also true that we are raised to think of that as perhaps an unhappy ending, one we might not choose if we had the choice.

I don't love maple syrup, but my sister does, and when my family moved back to Connecticut from Los Angeles, she was excited not just to be able to make maple syrup and taste it as it came out of the boiler, but to also embrace everything our family had in abundance: land, cousins, fresh air. I, on the other hand, was devastated, and eschewed what we had at the ready, every chance I got.

When a friend of mine had her second child, she asked her husband why her first was angry at the baby. She understood why he might be upset about change, and therefore upset at them, but she didn't understand why he actually hated his new brother, and her husband said: "all of life is a fight for resources, and now he has half of what he had before." It occurs to me now that it's not simply a fight for resources, but also whether or not we can accept and appreciate the resources we have available to us, the ones we have at the ready.

When I first tried maple syrup from the boiler, I took it down in one gulp, just as my sister had. I hated the feeling and the taste, but I said it was delicious and smiled. Then, I threw the plastic cup away.

Right: Timothy F. Phillips, "Corner of the Hemingway House," 24x24, acrylic on canvas, 2019.Laura Johnson

ROBERT L. PENICK

The Things We Don't Get Over

Like the ankle sprain in high school
that returns in your fortieth year
or the ex-lover who pops up
in the obituaries when
you are grayer than ghosts,
we have these records sorted and
filed away, of every bruised bone
or wounded heart, each exhibit
cataloged and boxed, stashed,
only to find them spilling out
to us, like the memory of your
first dog, years ago,
scratching at the door,
wanting back inside.

LAURA JOHNSON

in the garden

i did not plant tomatoes this summer; i think this is what dis-
turbs me the most.
steaming hot, fresh from the garden - from my hand – there
were no
  sweet tart rounds to offer you.
these ninety days marked a darkness of soul, a peculiarity in
spirit entwined
  by weedy roots that conquered the raised bed.
now i may not forage to find sun, wind, rain, soil contained in
an imperfect late season
  globe.

i'm guilty of non-planting.

i await my sentence.
a holy requirement willfully ignored deprived us of our ex-
pected
  caprese and fried greens –

i am to blame.
heirlooms – glorious in rainbows – did not stretch out branch-
es.
  no cherries or grapes
      to pop

in the children's mouths
when
they visited.
a wondering wandering spring gave way to narrow doubt and
clouded vision.

i failed.
this nightshade is not malleable – smashed to the floor, a
bruise, a burst – unhealed,
   unhealable.
water soaked days and the fruit may have proved plump and
pleasurable.
   no keeping corner for the unrooted – is it lost if i never had
it?
i have burgled time of its rightful offspring,
      too late thoughts require absolution that will
   never come.

Jared

I'm a substitute for a high school art class
when a deep-eyed boy tells me
he saw my painting in a dream.

He says it in passing, in between
a fire drill and informing me that my fears
of bull riding are unfounded,

that you never get hurt the way
you think you'll get hurt,
and that lunch is an extra
15 minutes long today.

I can't tell if he is making things up,
if someone really broke into his house
and shot at him, whether
he saw that in his dreams too.

I can't tell if he's sleepy
or just sounds it, likes
scaring the new teacher
or just likes her—

but he speaks with a slowness
like daylight fading, like evolution,
like cleaning a gun with care,

uncoiling the slow remembrances
of dreams, of paintings, of bulls
that almost got him, but didn't.

CONTRIBUTORS

Alana Benson is a freelance writer living in Lander, Wyoming. Her work is reflective of location: Wyoming's Wind River Mountains, small-town Kentucky, Vermont in winter, and downtown Athens. She has been previously published in *BlazeVOX* magazine and the University of Vermont's literary journal *Vantage Point*, and has also published six non-fiction books ranging in subject matter from identity theft to birth control.

Carl Boon is the author of the full-length collection *Places & Names: Poems* (The Nasiona Press, San Francisco, 2019). His poems have appeared in many journals and magazines, including *Prairie Schooner* and *Posit*. He received his Ph.D. in Twentieth-Century American Literature from Ohio University in 2007, and currently lives in Izmir, Turkey, where he teaches courses in American culture and literature at Dokuz Eylül University.

Brendan Connolly's work has been featured by *Genre: Urban Arts, OPEN: Journal of Arts & Letters, Gravel Magazine* and elsewhere. He lives and writes in Salem, Massachussetts.

Claire Elliott is a painter who lives and works in Portland, Oregon. She received her MFA from The School of the Museum of Fine Arts at Tufts University in 2014.

Laura Gill is a writer, photographer, and editor. Her essays have appeared in *Agni, Electric Literature, The Carolina Quarter*, and *Entropy*, amongst others. She contributes book reviews to *Barrelhouse*, and edits nonfiction for *Hobart*.

Laura Johnson is poet in Eastern Iowa who serves as a co-editor of the online literary journal *Backchannels*. She is a graduate of the University of Iowa. Laura participates in performance poetry and leads writing workshops in her community. Her work has appeared or is forthcoming in *Rosebud, High Shelf Press, Prompt Press*, and *First Literary Review-East*.

Nam Nguyen is a multimedia artist who enjoys photography, writing, and music. He has been published in *Jabberwock Review*.

Deb Nordlie has lived in twelve states and four countries, married once, had two children, and taught English since dinosaurs ruled the earth. After a lifetime of writing assignment sheets, she's branched into life stories, believing "we are all novels filled with short stories and poems." Currently, she teaches English in adult school and scribbles away at the Great American Novel.

Robert L. Penick's work has appeared in over 100 different literary journals, including *The Hudson Review, North American Review,* and *The California Quarterly.* He lives in Louisville, KY, , with his free-range box turtle, Sheldon, and edits *Ristau: A Journal of Being.* In 2018, he won the Slipstream Press chapbook competition. More of his writing can be found at www.theartofmercy.net.

Timothy F. Phillips is a totally self-taught artist who painted before he could read or write. He has had many one-man shows in museums and galleries around the world, and his art is in many private collections of estates and corporations as well. He is presently living in Miami, Florida for the last 20 years, and works out of his studio on Miami Beach. For more, visit timothyfphillips.com.

Eric Roller is a college recruiter and educator who lives in Port Angeles, Washington. His passion is helping young people find their voices. He enjoys wood-working and being outside in the Olympic National Park. He is recently published in the online journal, *Mothers Always Write.*

Annie Stenzel was born in Illinois, but she has lived on both coasts of the U.S. and on other continents at various times in her life. Her book-length collection, *The First Home Air After Absence*, Big Table Publishing, was released in 2017. Her poems appear or are forthcoming in journals from *Ambit* to *Willawaw Journal* with stops at *Allegro, Catamaran, Eclectica, Gargoyle, Kestrel, The Lake*, and *Whale Road*. She lives within sight of the San Francisco Bay. For more, visit www.anniestenzel.com.

Chestnut Review

VOLUME 1 NUMBER 2 AUTUMN 2019

FOR STUBBORN ARTISTS

CONTENTS

Cover: Christy Sheffield Sanford,
"Pink Fog from the El Greco Cape Series,"2018

Introduction

And so, autumn. It has been a wild ride so far. We are more grateful than we can say to those of you who have left notes and wishes for our debut. And here we are with our sophomore effort. As I write this, the Review has processed over two thousand submissions, both free and paid, with no sign of stopping. We appreciate, as ever, you sending your best work to us.

This issue's release represents five months since our formation. We're pleased that on the whole, things have been working out as we planned--testament to a practical, realistic sense of the challenges inherent in starting a literary magazine. We were able to put out our first issue early, in July, and that's a good thing. We have many plans for the future, but you, as the artist, are at the heart of everything we intend to do. These pages would be nothing, empty and white, without your contributions, your creations, and your daring to send them to us despite all the barriers the world puts in the way. Though it is impossible for us to comment on every submission, please know that everything you send is read, considered, and thought over--which is one of the things I believe all artists wish for. We may not be able to feature everything in the magazine, but we will always give it our attention.

All seasons invite different types of reflection. Autumn's can be melancholy, and certainly there are elements of that in this issue's works. But also hope, and an acceptance that we think you will find enlightening.

Consider: **Kelly Wise** enthralls us with the tale of a single tree (and we should note that we received many tree-themed submissions given our journal's name, but this one stood out). **Terry Barr** captures the human foibles on display while tramping through Italy in "Florentine Circles." **Russell Rowland** perfectly depicts the Halloween ritual in "Putting Pumpkins Out." **Julie Allyn Johnson** describes a near-crisis at night in "The Orientation of Your Deathward Momentum." **Claudia Buckholts** renders a perfect slice of personality in "The Bicycle Messenger." **Sharon Suzuki-Martinez** presents a bird saved and a bird saving in "Rescue." **Stephen Toskar** creates a poignant meditation on returning home in "The Onion Harvest." **Shevaun Branigan** contemplates time and mortality in "The spring they found the lump, Frank collected wind-up watches, learning the art of their repair." **Gloria Heffernan** contemplates the limits of what can be taught in "Reflexology Lesson."

Our cover art, "Pink Fog Cape from the El Greco Cape Series," is by **Christy Sheffield Sanford**, and we are pleased to feature the paintings "Song" by **Villania Wen** and "Dissassociation" by **Daisy St. Saveur.**

We hope you'll spend time with all of these pieces, and appreciate them as much as we did. Until winter, then. Keep creating, and being stubborn about it all.

James Rawlings

Aspen

Our roots were entwined from my birth, Aspen and I.
I was her confidant, I knew her routine-
She knew most of mine.

She mostly talked to me in autumn afterlight,
When people forgot about both of us.
That suited me anyhow.

I think we were kindred in all ways except height.
She was always taller than me.
Always prettier, better.

On All Saints Day 1993, I vowed to not visit anymore.
She let me free-fall and break my femur.
Enough of childhood games.

November 2, 1993 I found an ax in the garage.
Father deemed her absolutely rotten.
We flogged her at her base.

I pressed a leaf from her into chapter four.

Florentine Circles

I

Street signs in Firenze hide. As we disembark from the train, people push by, rushing to somewhere they know. We know nothing, just a hotel, Kraft, like the macaroni-cheese product we bought for forty-nine cents when our children were small. We see the hotel on our group I-phone, an indistinct symbol. We see ourselves, a throbbing red circle. But we don't know which exit to take, up or down, east or west. It's cool and raining. We follow our throbbing selves, eyes down, single file. We are almost run down three times by scooters and Fiats. I still can't see the signs, and when I do find one, I don't know anything more than "Via Lorenza."

II

To access our room, we must go up one floor. The elevator fits one person with a suitcase comfortably, but three of us get in. When I look out from our window at the street below, more people are wandering. My wife and I will sleep on two twin beds pushed together with a noticeable gap in between—a gap big enough to fall through. Our daughter says "And look at my bed," a day bed with cushions. "It's like your grandmother's," I say. Her look says, "An old-lady-bed." She is kind, but twenty-five, sleeping in a room with her parents on a bed she can't

place. The bureau tries for art nouveau but needs painting. The
hair dryer works for only five minutes and tires.

III

We go exploring. We don't need a phone-map now because
we have no real destination. The beloved couple and their
daughter, whom we're traveling with, believe we need to see Il
Duomo. We pass plazas of late afternoon diners, those waking
from the long afternoon's sieste. We search for the one place
that has fresh gelato, cold bierre, something more than just
sandwiches, and find a café owned by two late middle-aged
women who speak to us in Italian as if we understand. The
sandwich we get is mainly bread with a thin layer of cheese.
The gelato is not fresh. The Moretti is cold and plentiful, the
cappuccinos, just the opposite. Our bill comes to thirty euro.

IV

We find Il Duomo. The entrance is dark, though many walk
through. "Who wants to go inside?" one of our friends asks. "I
do," our daughter says. "I'll go with you," I say, because I want
to be where she is. "Well," our friend says, "you don't know
the price yet, and anyway, you have those stairs to walk." We
look up at the dome tower. People stand out looking down
and out. I am afraid of heights, but feel uncomfortable backing
out. "I don't think so," my daughter shakes her head. We circle
Il Duomo, and on the opposite side, we find a leather store
owned by two Persians, the ethnic origin of everyone in our
party but me. We buy a leather purse for our other daughter,
who worries about us.

"It's my feeding time again," our friend says. We see a Magnum chocolate shop. My wife orders a dark chocolate bar with dark chocolate sauce topped with sprinkles of dark chocolate, a concentric circle of Magnum. "Dark chocolate is healthy," she insists. I try a bite, and feel as if I have fallen through a gap between two single beds. It begins to rain, and we must protect the leather, so we walk faster, heavier, once more in single file. Though it is only five o'clock, my wife greets everyone with "Buenos Noches." She knows where we are, or at least says she does. We pass Gucci, Zara, and many market stalls. In one, I see a plastic pink child's purse. It says "Ciao Bella," costs five euro.

VI

We pass a doorway to a small shop. An attractive woman stands in the doorway. In front is a scruffy black dog, a spaniel-hound mix. The dog seems friendly, or at least passive. I stop and let him or her sniff my hand. I miss my dog, whom I almost refused to leave in the days before our journey. I pet the scruffy dog's head. We have a moment. The owner smiles and then as my party walks on, she helps me by calling the dog to her. "Ciao bella," I say to the dog. He barks and runs back to me. Tail and body wagging, he circles my legs. I look at the owner. "He doesn't like to hear 'Ciao,'" she smiles. "Arrivaderci, then," I say as he quiets and considers my passing.

VII

The Uffizi gallery is sold out. Undaunted, we pay double the amount for a tour led by Firenzen art students. Our guide, Martina, tells us she is really from Sienna, Firenze's traditional enemy. The sign at the entrance says "Beware of Museum

Touts," meaning the ones guiding us. Martina says, "The one thing you must not lose is your ticket. There are two checkpoints at the beginning, one at the end. The end doesn't matter, because the worst that will happen is you will spend the night in the museum, pacing from hall to hall, while I am having my dinner." I am uncommonly afraid of disobeying any direct order, and we have paid 100 euro for this tour. My daughter says, "Should I hold your hand?"

VIII

At the first checkpoint, two of our group can't find their tickets. We wait ten minutes while the tall, white-haired husband searches through the same pockets that continue to produce nothing. He speaks sharply to his wife who, my daughter testifies, has undergone numerous facelifts. Martina finally intervenes with the guards and obtains two more tickets. "Now, please hold on to these." At the next checkpoint, the same man searches again though his pockets. This time, after only two minutes, he produces the duplicate pair. Later, despite Martina's warning, he stands too close to a Botticelli while shooting with his phone, and a siren blares.

IX

We checked our hotel umbrella in at the cloakroom, for long umbrellas may not exist where we are traveling. Martina says that Raphael stole from Leonardo and Michelangelo to paint his "own" Madonna and child. Martina prefers Michelangelo. Art is political, and so is its criticism. We thank her for the tour and proceed to exit through the bookstore. A sign says, "Cloakroom" but points ambiguously to our left. We retrace many steps, through hall mazes and Carvaggios, and then descend again. Other ambiguous signs appear. Finally my daughter sees the cloakroom and retrieves our red umbrella, though the clerk shows her others like it, abandoned by forgetful wanderers.

X

A crowd gathers before a two-story house on Via Dante Alighieri, a sign I see easily. It is his house. "I've taught *Inferno* many times," I say. "That's why I love you," my wife responds. "Because I teach Dante?" We pass a young American family. "Dante lives here," the wife says. "Who's Dante?" her husband replies. "Ughhh," she rolls her eyes, and then catches mine. I smile, so does she. My daughter sees the husband's sheepish grin. So many sheep here in Firenze, lost in the continuing rain. The next day, our flight is delayed; the incoming pilot cannot land in a thunderstorm. We lose connections, keep circling, and land days later in the Carolina summer, lost no longer but sweating still.

Daisy St. Saveur, "Dissasocciation"

The Orientation of Your Deathward Momentum

Two-fifteen in the AM,
my heart stops cold.

I sense hesitation,
those phantom fingers.
The fine adjustment
of my pink
chenille spread
as you wrangle the covers down,
slow and exacting,
over my exposed
ankles and toes.

My eyes flash-open
to a still and empty room.
A quarter-moon shines
through an arched transom
window, skyward just shy of
the three-bedroom ranch
across the street.

Curious about
the placement of constellations
I can neither name or identify,
I pull back the curtains,
search the night sky.

The feeder needs refilling.
I'll have to mow tomorrow.

I switch on the light,
grab my readers.
Settle in with
Pillars of the Earth.

Nothing's changed.

I make it
through the night
and don't die,
always a good sign.

Bicycle Messenger

A bicycle messenger races through
wet streets, bent over the handlebars,
athwart a racing saddle. Wind's his
enemy, his friend. Cars pile up,
the lockstep of evening nears, he
twists through a corridor left open,
arrives at a flame-colored building.
He carries a document wrapped
in plastic against rain, up carpeted
stairs, into an elevator, a wall of glass
from which he can look down over
the entire city, boats turning restless
in the marina, trees canted toward
water, brick rowhouses. When the
bicycle messenger hands over the
document, a white-gloved man says,
You came too late. It would be better
you had not come at all. The bicycle
messenger lifts his racing goggles
to reveal a smooth face, a diabolical
look crouching in his pale eyes.
Nevertheless, he says, you'll pay.

RUSSELL ROWLAND

Putting Pumpkins Out

All-Hallows has forfeited its holiness.
Rolls of toilet paper hurled into trees
become pallid phantasmagoria, hang
like ghosts of the lynched. It is time
for decision about our pumpkins: set
them out on the steps, or keep them
in, like cats perching on windowsills.

Outdoors they will too easily become
someone else's pumpkins, our stoop
vacant at sunrise. Or else we waken
to find smashed shards of orange on
the road. Such tricks are not a treat.
Still, we've dared the banality of evil,
the wretches who kill from boredom.

They opened fire in schools—but we
will see our young ones onto the bus.
In churches—but we will lay our gift
upon the altar. In hospitals—yet we
will continue to visit the bed of pain.
We set pumpkins, just as vulnerable,
outside beneath the guardian moon.

Rescue

"Remember, Hope is a good thing, maybe the best of things, and no good thing ever dies."

–Stephen King

In the palm of my hand, the hummingbird looked up at me with the calm of a summer night. Encountering such trust always melts my jaded heart; lures my inner mother bear out of her cave.

The exhausted Anna's hummingbird had become tangled in rope of spiderwebs. Hummingbirds like to pluck bugs from webs like hors d'oeuvres served up on paper lace doilies. But this hummingbird's soiree had almost turned into a death trap.

Resting in my hand, she felt like a dandelion puff roiling with concentrated energy. Hummingbird hearts beat 1260 times per minute, 12 times faster than human hearts. To power such an engine, she must eat about 7 times an hour, or starve to death.

I fed her by dipping my finger in sugar water and offering it to her beak. She drank instantly—with a tongue I could feel, but not see. A few sips later, she zipped out of sight.
Far into the night, her optimism ran through my veins like lightning.

The hummingbird continues to flirt with death amongst our garden's spiderwebs. I look at her perching on her favorite branch, pausing from her hunt for bug amuse-bouches and pomegranate flower nectar. She looks back at me.

What is the word for the crazy hope you feel at sunrise, that morphs into hope that cries in its beer by noon, pierces its own heart in the evening, and heals itself overnight to gloriously resurrect every morning? I believe the word is hummingbird.

SHEVAUN BRANIGAN

The spring they found the lump, Frank collected wind-up watches, learning the art of their repair

5 o'clock, the notes read, *2 cm from areo*la.
Frank held my wrist to his ear to hear the ticking.

The tension in winding the crown of a watch
is sudden--I tell you, the lump
was nothing.
                Before release,
we sat in the waiting room,
listening for my name to be called.
Frank checked his watch, worried
it had stopped. Twice,
he offered to get me water.

Inside the machine, my breast clamped,
arms about the machine's casing,
fingers stretching past the wall
to Frank, scrolling through

the auction sites, looking for the broken lecoultre,
or a stout and sturdy tank missing its band,
the moon phase and its perpetual night,
the diver and its stuck bezel,
a cracked crystal,
the paused red second-hand.

The technician told me when
to hold my breath, the machine a movement
around me.
     Frank, the night before,
had held gears in tweezers, placed serrated gold
in my palm. It wasn't,
and I say this with confidence,
that he was trying to fix me;
the timing was coincidental.
We were in bed,
flanked by tables coated in watch parts,
their tools, resting on books on watch repair.
We lay there in silence,
his fine fingers touching my breast,
and because there wasn't any ticking around us,
I was grateful
for this fractured sense of safety;
this absence of time.

The Onion Harvest

I exit the highway at the off-ramp nearest Okadama Airport and turn at the first traffic signal, driving beside a dimly lit runway that disappears into farmland shadows. A metallic bitterness lingers at the back of my tongue from the black coffee I'd left in the cup that morning. Then an unexpected sweetness from the grounds. I feel my hands relax on the steering wheel now that my headlights are the only illumination on the road. It took three years to find this route, navigating the maze of countryside asphalt with only a dashboard compass, unable to read Japanese maps or afford a GPS. Then as the headlights snare in drifting smoke, my fingers clench and go numb.

The four-month snows come in a month, but in the morning you can already see long greenhouse tunnels where the onion farmers have begun tilling orange soil rich brown with compost from manure and straw, stretching vinyl sheets over metal pipes stuck in the earth like the exposed ribs of prehistoric beasts. In March the skin will glow a faint neon green, and then they'll peel it back in May so their tractors can scatter onion seedlings over bare fields like wilted pine needles.

The smoke clears on the curves and my lights pick out wooden crates with onions curing inside them in the cold, 1½-meter cubes of weathered slats on a side, stacked three high down a long tractor path, blue tarps tied to the tops. But I have to look twice driving through haze rising from the onion harvest's smoldering debris as my lungs fill with smoke reminiscent of maple leaves several months before I turn four. My sister and I are raking leaves into piles, waiting for an adult with a lighted match. I'm also waiting to be scarred for life when her bamboo rake's teeth expose another side of loss hidden within the flaming color of maple leaves before burning, when both cupped hands also fill. At odd moments I see her rake inscribe that same arc in slow motion. Then I touch the scar furrowing my left brow and listen to my mother scream in our foyer. It was impossible to explain then – still difficult today – but my own blood was all the proof I needed that beauty lay concealed inside me.

I follow winding roads out of Okadama, far past the local airport and smoke, then hit a wall of fog, not uncommon in late fall, that lasts through Shinoro and into Tonden – a single narrow bridge before coming into Hanakawa and feeling my hands again. The kids squeal and search my briefcase for gifts, returning empty-handed and sullen to the TV . . . mistaking me for a delivery man at the wrong house?

You barely lift your eyes from the dishes, then nod toward my covered plate of food. Your first streak of gray hair is shining in the light of a 60-watt bulb over the sink – fine trickles of milk spilling over black rock. You ask if I know what time it is, just a bit louder than the splash of dishwater. There is no way to answer such sadness.

I'll bathe the kids and put them to bed. Later, on the futon, the cool shock of your back against my stomach, the warmth of your breasts in my hand, if it is not already too late, I will try to peel the years, one layer at a time, down to another awakening of your weary skin.

Villania Wen, "Song"
24x24, acrylic on canvas, 2019.

Reflexology Lesson

Take a firm hold of the foot.
Slowly apply pressure.
Listen to the foot's response.
When it twitches or jerks
it is telling a story.

Though your hands
will never leave the feet,
you will touch every part of the body,
every crevice and appendage,
every nerve and muscle.
You must think of it
as a sacred act.

Don't worry about incense
or candles or music.
Let the rhythm of the breath
fill the room.
It is music enough.

When the client thanks you,
and says she has never felt better,
don't let it go to your head.
You can cure nothing.

You only provide a quiet space
for the body to heal itself—
if only for a little while.

Take meticulous notes.
there will come a time
when it will be important to know
that your right thumb
pressing the reflexes along the
anterior ridge of the left foot,

helped bring thirty minutes
of dreamless sleep to the client
who was tormented by insomnia
in the months before she leaped
from the 11th story window.

CONTRIBUTORS

Terry Barr's essays have been published in *storySouth, The New Southern Fugitives, Under the Sun, Coachella Review,* and *Lowestoft Chronicle,* among other journals. He lives In Greenville, SC, with his family, and blogs at medium.com/@terrybarr.

Shevaun Brannigan's work has appeared in such journals as *Best New Poets, AGNI,* and *Slice.* She is a recipient of a Barbara J. Deming Fund grant, and holds an MFA from Bennington College.

Claudia Buckholts has received Creative Writing Fellowships from the National Endowment for the Arts and Massachusetts Artists Foundation, and the Grolier Poetry Prize. Her work has appeared in A*laska Quarterly Review, Indiana Review, Minnesota Review, New American Writing, Prairie Schooner, The Southern Review,* and other journals; and in two books, *Bitterwater* and *Traveling Through the Body.*

Gloria Heffernan's poetry collection, *What the Gratitude List Said to the Bucket List,* is forthcoming from New York Quarterly Books. She has also written two chapbooks, *Some of Our Parts* (Finishing Line Press), and *Hail to the Symptom,* due out later this year from Moonstone Press. In addition, her work has appeared in over fifty journals including *Chautauqua Literary Journal, Stone Canoe, Columbia Review,* and *The Healing Muse.*

Julie Allyn Johnson enjoys long walks in the woods with her puppy, riding her bicycle, travel, photography, crochet, and hiking in the Rocky Mountains with her husband where they hope to bag a 14er this fall. Her poetry has been published in *Lyrical Iowa, Persephone's Daughters, Typishly, The Esthetic Apostle* and *Coffin Bell* with work forthcoming this fall in *The Loch Raven Review.*

Russell Rowland is a seven-time Pushcart Prize nominee and has two chapbooks with Finishing Line Press. A full-length collection, *We're All Home Now,* is available from Beech River Books. He writes from

New Hampshire's Lakes Region, where he has judged high-school Poetry Out Loud competitions.

Sharon Suzuki-Martinez's first book, *The Way of All Flux*, won the New Rivers Press MVP Poetry Prize for 2010. Her work has recently appeared in *Gargoyle, South Dakota Review, Duende, Okay Donkey*, and elsewhere. She was a finalist in the 2018 Best of the Net anthology, was awarded a residency to the Anderson Center at Tower View, a fellowship to Kundiman, grants from the Arizona Commission on the Arts, and a scholarship to the Fine Arts Work Center in Provincetown. Originally from Hawaii, she now lives in Arizona.

Stephen Toskar is a longtime US expat resident of Japan. His work has appeared in *Exposition Review, Arc Poetry Magazine, Chattahoochee Review, The Pedestal Magazine, LA Progressive, Hollywood Progressive, Tokyo Poetry Journal, Dissident Voice,* and *Poetry Nippon*, among others, as well as in the anthologies *Sixty Four Best Poets of 2018* (Black Mountain Press); *Enough* (Public Poetry, forthcoming); *Manifestations* (The D'arts Literary Anthology); and *Farewell to Nuclear, Welcome to Renewable Energy* (Coal Sack Press). He co-translated *Selection from Mother Burning and Other Poems: Parallel Translation of Selected Poems of Soh Sakon*. Living on the northern island of Hokkaido, he is a professor of English at Hokkaido Bunkyo University in Eniwa.

Villania Wen has been painting for several years, and has used her studies in biology and medicine to merge with her love of art and music to create inspired images meant to evoke a sense of calm and nostalgia, as well as a dreamlike quality through images. She was born in China and is studying medicine in Chicago after graduating from the University of Virginia in 2018.

Kelly Wise is a young author mostly interested in writing free-styled poetry and short stories. Her goal for everything she works on is to produce something meaningful. She wants to show people that there is always a hidden purpose to every word, especially in works by the next generation of authors.

Chestnut Review

Volume 1 Number 3 Winter 2020

FOR STUBBORN ARTISTS

CONTENTS

Cover: Erin Schalk, "Mineral Excavation"
Acrylic on canvas, 12" x 9", 2016

Introduction

Winter is upon us. We hope you can take a moment as 2020 begins to explore this issue's authors. Consider: **Aashika Suresh** instructs us beyond the literal and obvious in "A Career in Teaching." **Katrina Monroe** reflects on our namesake in "The Chestnut Tree." **Mary Buchinger** explores the resonances of a crash in "Route 83." **Yasmin Mariam Kloth** deftly captures the joys and challenges of childhood and parenting in "Daughter: Five Poems." **Jennifer Brown** depicts a culture of tobacco addiction in "Boys Will Be Boys & Girls Girls, They Said." **Siamak Vossoughi** captures nuances of dedication in "Thank You For Your Service." **Cynthia McVay** examines the space between affluence and pretense in "Perfect." **Katherine Szpekman** takes us inside attraction in "First Kiss on Riverside Drive." **Kevin Burris** observes salesmanship in "At the Optical Shop." Our cover art, "Mineral Excavation" is by **Erin Schalk**, and we are pleased to feature the photograph "Tide pool, Broom Point, Gros Morne National Park, Newfoundland" by **Richard LeBlond** and the painting "Spirit Wave" by **Britnie Walston**.

We hope you'll spend time with all of these pieces, and appreciate them as much as we did. Until spring, then. Keep creating, and being stubborn about it all.

James Rawlings

A Career in Teaching

The day I become an educationist, I will not teach the Pythagoras theorem or the right way to punctuate (though you ought to know when a semicolon is used and not a full stop).

I will teach kids things I wish I didn't have to teach myself. For instance, yesterday, I learnt how to keep my breakfast down in the middle of town after sudden clammy palms and an erratic heartbeat.

I will teach them how counting the cracks on the side of the pavement or skipping to maneuver the edges on the road can keep you from imagining your loved ones dying. At least for a little while.

I will teach them to look for a red van delivering posts across town, peer out their vehicle window and imagine grabbing a lost letter finding its way home to them for every phone call their lover rejects.

There could be days you will lie curled up in bed, exhausted, I will tell them, for so long that you may miss class or the train, or an important meeting, but sleeping in for just a bit more may mean saving your life.

You will make mistakes, I will tell them, such grave ones that you'll go searching every drawer you can find for a magical eraser that could wipe them right off. Or you'll go researching a time machine.

(Maybe you will build that time machine.) Either way, you can revisit the past over and over again, but what's done will be done, and you will have to live with the consequences, I will remind them.

You will sink to the ground, but you sure as hell don't have to stay there, I will say. Or hang your head low, thank heavens for the sternocleidomastoid and splenius muscles that help it defy gravity!

Find a beverage or a food, maybe a favourite poem or an object that fits in the palm of your hand that can serve as your talisman, I will tell them kindly, for days you cannot bear to live on.

It's a long journey, this life, and the mitochondria will keep its powerhouse going even if a person momentarily forgets how it does so. But on days when you are certain the world is conspiring for your downfall,

I will tell them, hold your breath for twenty counts and then go out seeking fireflies. For you see, science can teach you how sunlight angles through a prism, but you will need to learn how to catch its glint for yourself.

The Chestnut Tree

There was a survivor tree
in the yard of my childhood home
whose branches draped low and
whose top soared past my bedroom window,
oblivious to the pernicious parasite that felled its brethren.

In spring the abundant leaves
flaunted an effusiveness of flowers
forty feet of messy but majestic blooms,
the only reason for the tree's continued existence in Mom's opin-
ion.
The blooming period was followed by the sprouting period
where the hard won grass on that shady section of the lawn
was invaded by seedlings, sprung from roots,
vanquished week after week
by a lawnmower on a commando mission.
In the fall, chestnuts in gleaming browns
matching my dog's soulful eyes,
were pried from their spiky shells
scooped by the bucket full,
and used as gems to decorate my dresser,
as markers to play games,
even as students to play school.

On cold nights these precious gifts could be roasted,
destroying their beauty but yielding their nurturing, nutty softness.

Four decades later, from 3000 miles away, I was drawn back
to that house of 100 plus years,
standing strong, resplendent in its new paint job.
But it was standing alone, the chestnut tree was gone,
the house's stature, the eager joy in my heart, both diminished.
Did I expect that time would treat my survivor gently?
Beauty is not a defense against deterioration,
nor memories a bulwark against the reality of loss.
I peered over the hedge,
imagining I could find seedlings under the snow.

Route 83

That day in February
skiing cross-country
Suicide Bowl all morning early
afternoon in the glorious geography of risk
sun shattered with pines thick
by the trail and I barely twenty followed
my teacher and all the others learning
to lay down tracks snow-gold
light turned winter red   I bled
through cramps and blood
first of the day's surprises
back to the dorm I thought
half an hour drive shower and change—

then   I turned left at the blinking
yellow and the skis flew past my head
windows diamonded Fiesta back seat
snug-up against my gearshift but I
got out. And the old man said
You'd better call
  pointing
to the gas station on the corner

so I did and he was gone   cops
shook their heads
We're taking you
to the hospital
    But I'm fine I said
I just need to shower and they said
You don't even know what hurts
car totaled and I felt such shame
cramps and blood   Later

they find pieces of my car in the cracked grill
of the old man's pickup truck parked
in front of Toivo's Bar but I was
the college student out-of-towner
and he the town drunk
Sally's father
they said   Then a hearty laughing
orthopedic surgeon told me my neck
would be a problem the rest of my life
but my boyfriend of a month nursed me
carried plates of pork chops and eggs up
to me in his squeaky-spring bed
and how to make love in a brace
was my earliest and first the next year we
married   thirty-some years ago and I still
don't wonder what if

Daughter: Five Poems

Here

My daughter is the German-Polish border
that moved across Danzig. She's
the old stone castles of Irish fields.
My daughter is the city of Palmyra
before its columns were destroyed. She's
the white sands of the Sphinx. She's a mountain
in Beirut made of Cedar groves.
My daughter won't know Arabic in the way
I heard the language split French phrases
in my parents' house. She won't know the German
her father's forebears whispered
when the night would rock their ship
from sea to here.
My daughter's hair is soil in sun,
her skin an almond shell. Her eyes
are olive branches, her lashes shade.
My daughter laughs the way
the sky sounds just before it rains. She

cries in riverbeds where the rocks
have gone soft.
My daughter speaks.
When my daughter speaks
her voice is a wildflower planted

far from here.

At the Fountain

It's your favorite place
in the little town square,
this mossy fountain
surrounded by green
bushes and wooden benches.

It's our routine the two of us,
when your father is traveling
and the weather warms,
to buy an ice cream
on the corner with sprinkles
and little candy eyeballs.
You eat the eyes first,
then worry you've destroyed
the face already melted
in the sun.

We sit by the fountain with our
single scoops in hand

you ask me why you feel
rain on your face.
I tell you it's the fountain
spitting water when
a breeze blows by.

I didn't hear you at first
when you asked me
if there was a bird in the water.
Your words brushed past me
a spider web on a walk
through the woods.
Your words brushed past me
until you asked again.
I knew without looking.
I knew in the way the tiny hairs
on our skin will tell us things
about a person, a place, a dream.

I peered over your shoulder.
The bird on its belly,
its wings spread
as if it were human
with arms stretched
to embrace a friend.
You stared at the scene
questions in your eyes.
I took the cotton of your sleeve
and pulled you away.

I thought how close we are
to all of this, to the way we

can lose things
like the life of a bird
while we're eating ice cream
in the sun.

A Letter to My Daughter on Her First Day of Kindergarten

You stood behind a yellow line
painted in the pavement.
This, we told you,
was the safest place to wait.
You watched the yellow bus
pull up against
a yellow summer sun.
You crossed the line without us,
crossed the street without us,
backpack hanging on your body,
how is it possible your body
looks both small and big.
Your hand left the end of the skin
of my hand.
Today I learned:
There are places where we can't follow you.

We can tell you to be everything:
strong, kind, brave, thoughtful, tough--
when needed.
We can tell you our love follows
like a magician's cape, tell you
how it trails the halls behind your feet.

We can tell you our stories of this time
when we were young and
summer stretched like thread
into short nights and humid mornings.
We can tell you we didn't know
it would all pass so quickly
and how we send the children
we once were
to cross the line with you.

The day ended and changed
the morning light. I stood in the shade
 of the stop sign and the pines.
You stepped off the bus a small face
on the other side of the street.
Head right. Head left. Then running.
Your hand found the end
of the skin of my hand.
I didn't have to tell you anything.

You told me everything
that was new.

Normal

Sometimes I wonder if
my hugs should
feel this hard, this tight, wonder
if it's normal
to grab on like time
is running out,
or running fast, wonder
if it's normal I
keep my hands on
these small shoulders for
one more moment.
One more moment
buys me time,
buys me a second,
buys me a lightning strike,
a snowfall.

I hug you so hard I hear
you thinking,
what's wrong with you, why
do you squeeze me so hard,
stop it Mama that hurts, your
love hurts.
I'll trip over my tongue
to explain
patience and goodness and kindness
I'll trip over the words and what
they mean.

These days I feel
I cannot be
your teacher when
I fall short on all these things,
when I need to practice more
kindness and patience
in this wide open,
angry,
hot poker
world.

I cannot teach what
you already are.
I look into your fresh face and wide eyes.
I stop talking so I may see you, so
I may hear how you are all the words
I have been trying to say.

Daughter

For EJ

I am not equipped to pull this house apart.
The only tools what I found in the garage—the saw and the
leaf blower, the pickaxe,
and the tree limb cutter.

I am not equipped to pack up all the things that do not belong
to me. They were left for me to sort in piles (Throw, Give,
Keep)
years after she died—Chinese fans and masks, painted blue
ceramic cups, a teapot.
Gifts my father carried from his travels in his suitcase for her.

I do not remember most of these things.
Even after I've touched them for the first time
in many years, things that were the color and character in the
stories I'm sure she told at parties,
and her friends would laugh loudly through their drinks
and their happy tears.

I am not equipped to handle the heat of this pain, each thing I
touch a hot poker
and my hands raw.

Not all of this belongs to me, but I am daughter. I am duty and
honor and the keeper of things.
I will break this house down with my hands so it may breathe
again.

So it may breathe from beneath all the things I have never
seen before
but now,

how can I live without.

S I A M A K   V O S S O U G H I

Thank You for Your Service

It was on the Geary bus, getting on at 25th Avenue was a soldier in full uniform, not a thing you see every day in San Francisco, but you could still love San Francisco for the way that each day it gave you something you didn't see every day.

The soldier moved down the aisle and the man sitting in front of me came to attention. He looked like old San Francisco. These guys who are proud of San Francisco's progressive history, but to a degree. I had a soft spot for them because of Denny and Lon, two guys I would see at the Royal Ground. They were old-time San Francisco Sunset District guys and they would tell me stories from their boyhood and youth. Denny had been in Vietnam and I always remembered how he told me that if America ever had a draft again, he would send his son to Ireland. He had such a wonderful fire when he said he would send his son to Ireland, and then a great sorrow when he said his son would probably fight him on it. I missed the hell out of those guys.

The man sat up straight when the soldier passed him.

"Thank you for your service," he said.

The soldier smiled and I hoped the man would go back to looking out the window, because then I could trust his words at least and I could imagine he might be a guy like Denny, someone who actually knew what war was and had respect for a soldier but would still send his son to Ireland if he got drafted, but the guy didn't do that at all, and instead he looked around to see who'd heard him, as if to challenge them, as if to say, I know this is San Francisco, but it's America before it is San Francisco, and the thing to do when you see a soldier in uniform is to thank them for their service. And I had just a flash of a moment when his eyes met mine that I thought his words might be directed at me, an Iranian man, and for just a moment it unlocked the part of me that worried every day that America is going to attack Iran, and I'm going to hear people thanking soldiers for their service of attacking my country, and then how the hell am I supposed to live in America, let alone write American stories that sing? But somehow the memory of Denny and Lon saved me, because I knew those guys, and the guy reminded me so much of them in the way he was trying to say that San Francisco was still the San Francisco of his boyhood and youth, and he had a desperation in his eyes that made me think he would've said it and looked around the way he did whether I was there or not.

Still, I went traveling through all my different ages when he said it like that, to my own boyhood and youth, when I would have felt it was directed at me, when I would have understood it as the voice of authority, an authority that I did not necessarily want to fight against, as much as I wanted to fight against the notion of war as service, because I liked service. I did not have the first thing against service, but I looked around me and thought, we're not possibly that scared, are we, to think that war is the only service? Because what do you do if you like service but hate war? Well, you can write stories that you hope can be of some service. I wrote a short story collection called *Better Than War*. I wished I could give a copy of it now to Denny and Lon, but I had been out of touch with them for a while. I wished I could give a copy of it to the man who'd thanked the soldier for his service. Here, I'd say, this is just to balance things out. That would be nice. I'd probably be too scared to do it if I had a copy with me. You got a problem with the American soldier? he'd say to me. No, but I got a problem with war, I'd say. Maybe then he would say, Me too, and then we could look at each other and angrily agree with each other. I like to think that I could get to the point of angrily agreeing with anybody. That's what I was trying to do with the stories in the book. I was trying to say that a bunch of American soldiers and a bunch of Iranian soldiers shouldn't kill each other, because there are magnificent lives that Iranians are living and there are magnificent lives that Americans are living as well. Every story can be an anti-war story, in my opinion, if the lives of the people in those stories are shown to be wonderful. I had no doubt just then that the life of the solider on the bus was wonderful, and that the life of the man who had thanked him for his service was wonderful. He had all of San Francisco, for one thing, new and old, and he was in the struggle of trying to make a straight line between his present and his past, which was a beautiful struggle to be in. I didn't have an idea for the next story I was going to write, but I looked around the bus and thought, it has to be something that is talking to all of the people on this bus. It has to be something that is talking to all of them, written in plain language, with no tricks and only very humble flourishes.

That was a good start for now. Keep them all in mind when you sit down to write, and something will grow out of that, I told myself. Keep yourself in mind too, and laugh about the funniness of an Iranian man writing stories that Americans will recognize as their own, as coming from a place inside them that they didn't know was there. Laugh because it is funny. Even if it is only funny today and might be any number of things tomorrow. A writer has to put a great deal of faith into today anyway.

I got so lost in my own thoughts that I almost didn't notice that among the passengers getting on at 10th Avenue was a Buddhist monk. I used to pass by their temple when I lived over there on Funston. He walked toward the back and then a young white kid, whom I hadn't noticed till now, turned to him and said, "Thank you for *your* service."

The kid didn't look at the soldier, or at the man who'd thanked him for his service. He went back to looking out the window, like he was carrying war and peace inside him before he'd said it, and he would be carrying them after.

That's how you thank someone for their service, I thought.

The monk smiled, like he'd known for a long time that life was already happening before he stepped into any particular moment of it. He sat down next to the soldier, who moved over to make space for him in the back row.

The man who'd thanked the soldier for his service looked like he wanted to say something, but the kid made it clear that he was done, that he'd said his piece, and anyway all it was was balance. You couldn't say the monk hadn't been of service, and you couldn't say he didn't deserve to be thanked. Anyway the solider had gotten a kick out of the whole thing, and the man couldn't say anything without showing that what he was actually reaching for was his own boyhood somehow, and I wished him luck that'd be able to find it some other way, and I loved the hell out of San Francisco for wearing its heart on its goddam sleeve, for wearing its heart on all its goddam sleeves, and I told myself that if you can't make stories out of this city, it's on you.

K A T H E R I N E   S Z P E K M A N

First Kiss on Riverside Drive

You leaned in.
Our eyes closed.
While rain, a mist so light
we may have imagined it,
caught us in a fine net,
on iridescent pavement.

Tears of the gods spilled
from April's warmest breath.
Your lips, moist,
lustrous with liquor and
nacre, at the same time
both sweet and briny.

Our mouths, anticipatory,
opened like oysters in their beds,
and your tongue swished in
like sea water,
in and out,
searching for a pearl.

Britnie Walston, "Spirit Wave"
Acrylic on canvas, 10" x 20", 2019

Perfect

You meet Barbara in Central Park when Charlotte is a round puppy. Barbara is part of the morning Labrador group, the group you saw by the reservoir one day when you decide that's what you want: a Labrador. Your puppy is one year younger than everyone else's by the time you join but you are now part of the group. The group is an eclectic mix whose only common feature is you all own Labradors, although perhaps that choice may imply some commonality. For example, you did not get your dogs at the shelter or save them in the streets of Accra when you were Peace Corps volunteers. This is a group who as individuals sought out breeders and found dogs with pedigree. You never mention that you found Charlotte in the backyard of a trailer in the Hudson Valley and she was next-to-runt of a 13-puppy litter. She does have papers, and you prefer her long legs and slender body to the squat English Labradors anyway.

You are welcomed into the group which includes the sommelier of Le Cirque restaurant, who owns two thick black Labs of different ages. He always has a good story to tell, or gossip, like the time he saw Martha Stewart and Donald Trump dine together. He also confirms, as you suspect, that all the slender young gorgeous women at the bar are Russian prostitutes.

The group also includes the entertaining and charming wife of a European diplomat with a Field Labrador like your own Charlotte. She, too, is a font of inside information of the global political kind. She tells the group, laughing, about how her handsome son gets blow jobs from the girls in his private school on the Upper East Side; you cringe because your fourteen-year-old daughter doesn't talk as much to you as she used to; you are glad she is at a different school. One morning, after W is president, Diplomat's wife tells the group how, when they raided Saddam Hussein's palace seeking weapons of mass destruction, they found a closet full of Botox and blackberry jam. It is unclear whether the Botox is to treat Hussein's vanity (photos reveal a deep worry crease in his forehead), blephoraspasm, (eye seizures—the original reason Botox was invented), or, in fact, is to be considered bacterial warfare, given its paralyzing features. No one can or cares to explain the stash of blackberry jam.

In the group tangentially is a flabby-faced, argumentative younger woman lawyer who always wears leggings and is having a hard time conceiving. She tells you how to lose weight and you wonder why she feels she has the right to do so, why she is telling you her dieting tricks that don't seem to work. She is remarkably hard on her handsome, gentle husband who sometimes comes to the park with their Lab in her stead.

And then there's overdressed Barbara, vivacious and upbeat with her squat and big-headed English yellow Labrador. You both appreciate more than the rest of them the cherry blossoms in spring and the maple leaves in the fall and you *talk garden* because you both have country houses. She is an expert maybe over-the-top gardener, if the rest of her life is any indication. You have children roughly the same age who track.

It isn't clear whether Barbara and hers pretend to be the perfect family for everyone else or whether they really think they are, or they really are. Perfect in a number of ways. For one, there are four of them, one of each. A mother, a father, a daughter, a son. Barbara, Mike, Chloe, Christopher. Typical in the non-typical way, since these kinds of *typical* families rarely exist anymore; not perfect, yet something to shoot for. But perfect in that *we just got back from Paris* kind of way. More than normal. But they aren't normal, of course. The slight limp in Mike's gait tells a lot of the story, but not all of it. It is just a clue, a clue to approach slowly.

One by one, over the years, the Labrador group disbands. Diplomat dog is attacked in another setting and is never the same. Diplomat's wife was the glue, so the group is at risk. Le Cirque closes, and Sommelier moves to the country and opens a wine store. Flabby is not very interesting on her own, in fact she was never interesting, just angry, and so you and Barbara continue to seek each other out, find each other in the park every morning, and find ways to avoid Flabby.

By now, you know a lot about each other, given the therapy-like nature of the dog park dynamic, although your dogs don't interact much once they are adults. Charlotte is interested only in raiding baby strollers of bagels and cookies. *Sorry, sorry*, you say as you run to pull her away by the collar. You feign surprise, say *that never happens* but carry a five-dollar bill in your front pocket to whip out to compensate the irate parent of the shrieking child. Barbara's dog carries a tennis ball in his iron jaw.

Even though the unspoken rule dictates you don't see dog friends outside the park, you do, because you enjoy each other's company, and you are perhaps aspiring or lonely, so you let Barbara absorb you.

You hear a lot about Barbara's extraordinary family before you meet them. Her children are exceptional. Her husband is attentive, so good to Barbara. She tells you that on her birthday, and on Mother's Day, he makes her breakfast in bed. Brings her flowers. Takes her to a romantic dinner and a show. They are still in love. You believe her.

They hold a tree-trimming party every year. And a red-carpet Oscars party. You like to get dressed up once in a while but wonder why anyone would want to trim someone else's tree when you can't get anyone to trim yours. You find out that no one really trims the tree. You eat petite delectables from a silver tray and drink a lot and meet other rich thin people from New York, even though you are not rich nor thin.

The Serbian housekeeper, or a swift young man in a dark suit, opens the door, and takes your wrap and hangs it in the foyer closet. There is no *throw it on the bed* thing in their home. Someone, maybe Mike, steps forward with a flute and a bottle of champagne, immediately, offers you a glass. It is real champagne, too, not sparkling wine from Germany or prosecco. And there's lots of it.

Barbara bursts into the room with a smile, brimming, jubilant. That is, if she isn't still getting ready. You arrive early, *on the dot*, in part to be supportive, in part because you can't help yourself. Barbara is always late, even for her own parties. And you wonder, *how can someone be late for her own party?* Mike winks and nods, conveying this is part of her charm, that his bouncy wife, clad in, gripped by, some designer dress worth thousands of dollars, is still dolling herself up. You wonder whether there is tension behind closed doors.

And although not as svelte as many of her guests, like, say, the woman who was a principal in the New York City Ballet, Barbara looks fabulous. Just slightly red-headed with flawless, pore-less skin, which may have been touched up by the plastic surgeon who is Mike's best friend. Her halo of energy captivates you. Whatever is on your mind or concerns you, like the fact that she is late for her own party, vanishes, because her energy takes over the room, over you. She bubbles, champagne-like, about the tree or who will win best actor.

You don't really care that much about either, but you are seduced by her love of it all. You're not sure you like all the pomp and circumstance, all the gold, when she shows you the antique side table she has sanded and re-gilded herself. You'd back up your Volvo if you saw it in a pile on the street and whisk it away, but it is not your style. It doesn't really interest you, but it interests her, and she is proud of her work, so you *ooooo* and *ahh*, you run your finger along the edge, because you know you should, because it will make her happy. Even happier.

The tree is big and full. They picked it themselves and brought it home from the Catskills. The ornaments are her grandmother's, of course. With delicacy, Barbara hooks an antique reindeer onto the end of a bough as she tells you so.

Barbara made all the little canapes that afternoon, complicated ones with tiny sprigs of dill and pastry and cream and home-smoked salmon. Not just generous wheels of imported aged cheese with artfully tossed candied walnuts and dried cranberries, but there's some of that, too. And flowers, fresh aromatic, over-the-top bouquets and maybe even an entire sideboard of moss and flowering dogwood and lily of the valley.

Can that be true? She smokes her own salmon?

Everything is so perfect except that Mike walks with a limp and has the voice of a mobster.

You are surprised the first time you meet him because he doesn't fit Barbara's description. He has not quite a comb over and a hard edge and no sense of humor and will know more than you no matter what you talk about. You will never see him smile. He reminds you that he sculpts and shows you some of his pieces on pedestals in the living room which you think aren't bad. He will insist he is an excellent tennis player; you don't doubt him, but it is hard to contain your surprise given the laborious way he walks. It is clear that he has worked hard to overcome his childhood polio and the Bronx, all that he must have endured, and he wants everyone to know it has been full-steam ahead as a self-made man. That he loves the opera and appreciates fine food, he knows his wines, has his own driver and a place on Shelter Island and a sailboat.

Barbara and Mike take you out for dinner to fancy, sophisticated restaurants and night clubs, late at night, later than you are used to, in that New York way, which is not really your way. Their driver drives you home. Mike won't let you pay, so you reciprocate in other ways, by treating Barbara when it's just the two of you, say.

Mike and Barbara show you extraordinary hospitality. You are their third wheel, when you are not seeing someone, double date when you are. They set you up with Mike's plastic surgeon friend. Although he is smart and articulate, you have a hard time with his profession, what he stands for. He is not your type, and you are not his. You know you would be a project with your big nose and imperfect skin, and while some part of you is tantalized by the prospect of being perfect, too, it is against everything you believe in, what you scorn. You don't see each other again *in that way* and are polite when you see each other at future tree trimming or Oscaring and pretend to not know each other when either of you brings a date.

When you try to understand what Mike does, it never makes sense. He has a private investment business, a partner you never meet. He travels, he does deals. He owns or leases hundreds of thousands of acres in Papua New Guinea that he will clear cut to grow other things. You try to hold back outrage—you have been reading a lot about PNG because it is at the top of your bucket list—but he describes it in such a way that it seems he is saving the place. *What about the fragile ecosystems that host the intricate, unique birds of paradise and the peoples yet untouched by diet Coke?* Mike says he will set aside a certain amount as a reserve, which wouldn't happen otherwise. He will feed hungry people. He is saving PNG. He gives the biologists three months to do an ecosystem survey, which you know is a blink of time, nothing, to do meaningful research. He seems to care about the environment, but you don't see how what he says squares with what he does. You try not to ruffle feathers, but you may be operating in denial here, not wanting to know, knowing you can't change what he is doing. You contemplate boycotting them or ask Barbara about it. You will on other occasions try again to understand what he does, maybe when he arrives back from a trip, probe and plunder, but you never will feel comfortable about this. You wonder where you are supposed to draw the friends line.

You will never forget about the time the three of you go to a movie, a premiere. Mike secures tickets ahead of time, four great seats in the center, ten rows in from the screen. Four, so you can stow your winter coats in the extra seat. The theater lights dim. All the seats are occupied, so people arriving late keep asking *is that seat taken, the one with the coats?* And Mike says, in his gruff, mafia voice, "I bought that ticket." It just doesn't make sense to people, that he bought a seat, for $15, the price of a movie in New York, for coats. They are exasperated looking for a seat for themselves. It is one of those grey situations that no one is right, no one is wrong, but everyone's pissed. You are embarrassed but enjoy the luxury of not having to sit on your coat, and not having to fight for it, but it's unseemly.

Then there's Chloe, a perfect specimen, thin and angled, a vegetarian, of course. She remembers your name, greets you like an old friend, even though you are her mother's age, her mother's friend, because she wants to work where you used to work. She wears tiny dresses that cost thousands of dollars per square inch. You are surprised her bedroom is a tornado when you explore the apartment pretending to look for the bathroom. Shopping bags and tissue paper, bright pink lacy thongs and re- jected evening- wear are strewn across the floor, the unmade bed. She is just in from Paris or Rome or Boston.

You eventually find the bathroom, right where Barbara said it was, where it was last time, with a flickering candle obfuscating potential smells and softening the overhead light. The hand towel is plush-new.

Chloe, who speaks French and learned Italian because she now has a gorgeous, wealthy Italian boyfriend who thinks she is exquisite, is doing better now. All through middle school and most of high school, Barbara speaks of Chloe's academic prowess and exceptional SAT scores, record-beating track meets, ribbon-garnering horseback riding, the summer research jobs, and how she will go to Yale.

And then one day Barbara comes to the park looking tired and says that Chloe has been taken away during the night.

"Kidnapped?"

"We staged an intervention."

"What?"

"They came at four in the morning and handcuffed Chloe and took her away." There was screaming, a struggle.

This is the first you hear of Chloe's drug issue. That she had been running in the wrong crowds, which is easy to do in New York City, that she was out all night long clubbing and developing *a habit*. That it had gotten so bad and out of control and then came to a screeching halt all in thirty seconds for you is immaterial because it is not your story, but you are surprised you had not heard about any of this until this morning when it began and ended all at once.

"She is going to a farm in New Mexico."

Perfectly manicured, lace-thonged, rake-thin Chloe has a drug problem that will go away shoveling shit in New Mexico.

She will not go to Yale after all.

Her unexpected gap year will become her college essay, her learning, and she will go to Colorado College. She will somehow nip all those drugs in the buds and do well enough. She straightens out. She will work for her father. She is good at math and spreadsheets. She consults you about consulting.

Barbara confides in you that there is tension between Mike and her. Mike spoils Chloe, buying her handbags and fur coats, and anything else she wants. Is that before or after rehab, you can't remember.

And then there's Christopher, who is your daughter's age technically, but who acts like a middle-aged man. At the Oscars or tree trimming party he wears a long smoking jacket and velvet slippers with emblems. His hair is like his mother's, big and wavy with just a touch of red, a hint of Kennedy. He can talk about politics and the election, in Latin probably, better than most adults. He holds his own. He will go to Harvard, or Oxford. And maybe it is Christopher who is pouring the champagne one of those evenings, for one of those gatherings. He, too, remembers your name and who you are.

It is decided that Christopher will go to boarding school, where he can play more tennis and sail. He is a star tennis player, like his father. Mike's driver ferries Christopher to his tennis lessons in midtown twice a week. He is ranked, as he is in sailing. But over the summer, Christopher develops pain, excruciating pain in his wrists and legs. He takes a bevy of tests. His body is screaming, screaming in pain, screaming to stop. He stops.

He seems of a different era, and you can see why boarding school might be good for him, in that past-generation kind of way. Everyone's ecstatic but not surprised when he is accepted to one of the top schools. When they move him in, Barbara outfits his room like a Ralph Lauren showcase. The other students don't understand the velvet window treatments and oriental rugs. It seems pretentious, although it isn't clear whether it is pretention or the real thing. His thing. Them.

He is acing all his classes, so you hear, loving it, until one day, Barbara tells you in the park, that he is expelled from school for cheating. Inadvertent or deliberate, he has lifted whole paragraphs of Latin translations from the internet, and it is likely not the first time he has done so, but part of a concerning pattern.

Over the next few months, park conversations revolve around where a student goes after he's been caught cheating. What school takes him halfway through the year? God forbid, he goes to public school in New York City where he will probably be beaten up.

But there he is, back home not just for the Oscars or the tree trimming party but living again. And you are not sure how to interact with him but give him a polite kiss as you always have. He refills your glass. You think you might understand why he has cheated.

Somehow, they find another boarding school that will take Christopher. The school takes fuck-ups, kids who struck out in one way or another, so it's good that he will finish the school year, and high school, but not good because everyone—meaning colleges and anyone who matters—knows that's where fuck-ups go.

A couple months later, Barbara and Mike get a phone call from the school. Something is going wrong, even for fuck-up school. Christopher takes too many showers for the average bear. He wears his clothes for an hour or just touches them, and lets them fall to the floor, sullied. Barbara's plush towels are washed threadbare. He has no more clean clothes. He is naked, won't leave his room. When he comes home, he uses rolls and rolls of paper towels. He doesn't touch door knobs with his hands. A pile of slightly crumpled paper towels accumulates beside the bathroom door. He takes five showers a day, for an hour. Uses the towel once.

Barbara is at a loss. She is losing it. He is driving them all insane.

This goes on for months, until they rent an apartment for Christopher to live separately but nearby. He is now eighteen and hasn't finished high school. But he's finished 1,543 rolls of paper towels. Because he is emancipated, they cannot force him to take the medication. But because he is incapacitated they pay for his apartment. He only leaves his apartment to get more paper towels. He runs out of money and begins to steal paper towels. He gets caught stealing. He's cracked.

And then, in the middle of all this, there is more.

What you don't know, and Mike doesn't, and Barbara and they don't, is that there is something growing in Mike's head. At first it is just a blurry eye and then a splitting headache, and then within a week they, and you, find out that Mike has a tumor and he has less than a year to live. You find out because Barbara, who continues to come to the park even after her dog dies from eating a philodendron leaf, doesn't come to the park anymore.

You are with Barbara for that year, his last year, which is fraught with optimism and pain and canapes and tree trimming like all those before. Everyone raises their glass as if nothing is happening. The housekeeper grabs you when Barbara is out of the room to tell you how crazy everyone is, and how she wants to quit. But she is still there months later, even though or because her own husband is dying.

The landlords of the house they rent on Shelter Island don't renew their lease, which comes as a surprise to you for different reasons than for them. You thought they *owned* their house on Shelter Island. But it turns out they have rented that house for twenty years and Barbara decorated and gardened and planted a dozen trees that final year, and then the landlord pulled the house from under them.

Mike sues the landlords just before he dies. And then he dies. Not suddenly, because everyone is on notice, everyone is expecting it, but even so, when the moment comes it feels like a surprise. You feel badly for Barbara, of course, but cannot help but think and thank that maybe Papua New Guinea is spared.

The memorial service remembers Mike's love of opera and elegance, his love of Barbara. Somewhere in that man was a tenderness, a thoughtfulness. Tree-trimming and Oscaring party guests are in the pews in muted fare. Barbara's mother doesn't come to the funeral because Barbara's sister told Barbara not to burden their elderly mother with the news. You meet Barbara's sister who never liked Mike, didn't think Barbara should have married Mike. Barbara had many, many suitors that were more suitable and she should have settled for one of them. Barbara has told you that her sister is angry and bitter because she married late and never had children.

A couple days after Mike is interred, Barbara calls you at 7:00 AM from her car. You pick up, ready to console Barbara in her grief.

"I had to move everything out of the summer house. Yesterday, the movers filled a truck and my car. I'm selling the sofa and the sailboat." Barbara spent the night in her BMW X5 in Long Island on the side of the road. She laughs uncontrollably.

Ha, ha! She is always bubbly.

"Barbara, you should have called me!" You had no idea. Everything falls apart all of a sudden with Barbara. It's always over when she calls. You suggest slowing down. She accelerates.

Barbara finds out that Mike left no money, no funds, no health insurance. Taxes are due. There are enormous, unmanaged medical bills, and Christopher. Weeks earlier, Mike renewed the lease on their New York City apartment, which you also thought they owned. The rent is $13,000 a month, and you wonder why on earth they would renew *under the circumstances*, or any circumstances. You would never rent anything for that much money. But certainly not under the circumstances. But then you realize that is precisely why they re-upped the lease: It was their lease on Mike's life.

Overnight, his business goes *poof!* Gone because it was just him and his partner, a shell, and the partner's moving on, the invisible partner. Barbara is laughing and crying and wondering how she will pay rent. Her sister who has *all the money in the world* never liked Mike. Her sister won't lend her anything. She's such a bitch.

Barbara cannot even mourn with her own mother because she didn't tell her mother that Mike was dying, Mike is dead.

Why isn't Barbara angry at Mike for leaving her this mess? Did she know all along that the whole thing was a sham? She is smart and was in business before. She should have known. (You should have known. Did you?) They could have reigned it all in. And now she has the apartment and Christopher's rent to pay, debts, and not a dime, and she's emptying the twenty-year summer rental. It's all so exhausting and Barbara's laughing.

You remember all the money that was spent, the lavishness. The coat seat. You were part of it all. Barbara still has her full-time housekeeper. She perpetuates her lifestyle even as the sordid underbelly reveals.

The following week when you check in on Barbara, she is starting a jewelry line, maybe a lifestyle business. That's why she needs to keep her apartment. Everyone wants to be her, have her look, her life, she says. You buy a necklace from her to help, the cheapest thing you can find on her dining room table for $300, even though she tells you she marks things up by twenty times and you usually only buy things on sale or in the open-air markets of developing countries where there are no middlemen. You pretend to believe her when she says she designs this stuff herself, even though you have seen things just like it all over Asia. She travels to the Philippines a couple times a year to bring things back. She has trunk shows.

A year later, Barbara's mother dies. She leaves Barbara nothing, because she thinks Mike is still alive. That's when Barbara realizes that's why her sister told her not to tell her mother that Mike was dying, that Mike is dead. Barbara's mother wouldn't leave anything to Barbara as long as Mike was in the picture. Barbara's sister gets everything.

You come to the city for an event and suggest getting pedicures together but when you go to meet Barbara at her favorite place, she, of course, is running late, and it turns out to be one of those places that charge $50 for a pedicure, not $23, like the one you infrequently go to. You can't believe Barbara is still doing this, under the circumstances, actually it kind of outrages you, since Barbara has been hinting she could use a loan. You leave before she arrives, which is a half-hour after you were supposed to meet. You understand why her sister won't lend her money.

You want to help Barbara but now you know you can't. You try to remember the last time Barbara asked you about you.

Barbara tells you that Chloe gets a job offer at the place you used to work but turns it down for a firm that is second tier, and you wonder how that can be.

Barbara is very busy, and you know in part it is to avoid being still, sidestep the pain, the swirl of horror around her. She keeps up her champagne life because it is what she is selling. You check on her, keep up for a while, but over time, with less frequency. You *like* things she posts on Facebook. You visit her, drop in or meet for coffee when you can, until it seems less and less convenient and the lies are so overwhelming that you don't think you have much to talk about anymore. And you have tired of only listening. She doesn't even know who you are.

You have a hard time accepting that Christopher lives off a government disability program in Utah, the cheapest place Barbara could find for him to live on his own. He has a therapist who meets with him monthly. When Barbara drops by to visit him on her way to California for a trunk show where she will sell $100,000 worth of extravagance, he will not open the door. She laughs when she tells you and says it doesn't bother her. You wonder how it can not bother her, how she laughs.

You know that mental illnesses can be genetic. You wonder what the effect of living the gilded life, in a champagne bubble, in the cracks of truth, can do to a person. You find out that brain trauma can lead to Obsessive Compulsive Disorder—many football players develop it—but it strikes you as bizarre and ironic that the trauma to Mike's brain is manifest in Christopher.

The third anniversary of Mike's death shows up on Facebook to remind you of how things can go so wrong when everything seems so perfect, so normal. When everyone's smiling. You hover on the page and wonder what to write. You write nothing. You write this story.

Boys Will Be Boys & Girls Girls, They Said

Down south, like the banner of a borderless nation, the circle bleached in the backpocket of jeans gives away manhood's pledges. You can buy smokes at sixteen if you can't steal them from parents or bum them. I find my coworker's stashed forgotten on the topedge of the ladies'-room mirror for between-break breaks. Her name is Gayle. She's my mom's age or older, stunted, working stock at the drugstore when the pharmacist puts me on the register, younger & neater.

Around me, the women smoke & the men suck & spit, chipmunk-cheeked & buzzing. From women I learn the many forms of finesse, fine-motor fingers flipping the neat box open, the tinsel-sound of cellophane, the ritual tap of box on palm, flip & flip, the faint swish of one cigarette slid out to scissored fingers, slick-tipped with pale polish. A filthy habit, my mother says, but I can't agree, not when the trick of the lighter's toothed wheel makes flame & a glowing coal, a wand for punctuation & gesture as coils of smoke carry words & my grandmother's breath into the world. As, later, the smoke will carry her away, something finally other than a body.

But that is years off. For now, women breathe fire & men &
boys who want to be men however unimaginable that is at 14
or 16—those not-yet-men pack tobacco inside their lower lips
against teeth & gums, carry cokecans of warm brown spit from
class to class. They sit in Typing salivating for the teacher's
always-cleavage-baring dresses, her dark tan & bottle-blonde &
the cleft of her breasts keep them shuffling up to ask for a hall-
pass, leaning over her desk. The rest cock their chairs on two
legs back, spit hot juice in their cans or stolen cafeteria-cups,
sliding them into the desktrays below the typewriters.

Fathers chew & spit while mowing grass, cheeks distended—
as long as they keep it out of the house the mothers look the
other way, shooting jets of smoke out mouthedges to clear
their eyes. A girl, I do not learn to spit, can barely clear my
mouth of a bitter taste unless alone, where I don't have to hide
in napkin-manners, girl that I'm trying to be. I'm coached &
coaxed to avoid the legacy of swagger, the father-to-daughter
burden of longlegs as likely to hobble me with coltish clumsi-
ness as to charm my springing-up weed of a body to grace. I
learn instead to pucker my lips around the stem of smoke as if
to demonstrate, breath by breath, how I might kiss, what my
mouth can soon promise a man.

At the Optical Shop

The man in the monogrammed lab coat
starched and white with his head shaved,
looking all medical and a little like
a shady purveyor of ice cream,
is advising an older man and his wife
of the benefits, the manufacturer's claims
for each potential selection
on a looming mirrored wall of frames.

These, he is saying, *offer a classic look.*
Think Philip Larkin, think Jean-Paul Sartre.
Think British don in his Oxford rooms
puffing a Dunhill and lecturing
on the essential ornithology of the Amazon.

And these, he points out, *are titanium.*
Think spaceships, think robots, think
Arnold Schwarzenegger, indestructible
cyborg rising from the Sturm und Drang.
Think Q walking Bond through his secret lab,
pointing to an ordinary pair of glasses.

Now these, he says next with extra breath,
are designer, presenting them as a queen
presents a medal. Think Halston, think Gucci,
think Yves St. Laurent. Think about you
resplendent on your immaculate yacht,
the cliffs of Monaco to starboard,
young love immediately to port.

The old folks seem uneasy.
He is pulling at the patch on his injured eye.
She is fidgeting with a loose thread
hanging from the handle of an old fabric bag.
What they want to know is:
how much?
Think Medicare. Think furnace repair.
Think a single fast-food burger, split, for lunch.

CONTRIBUTORS

Jennifer Brown studied creative writing at the University of Maryland and University of Houston. She spent many years teaching college and high-school English, living on the campus of a boarding school, and teaching creative writing in summer programs. In 2018, she won the Linda Flowers Literary Award from the NC Humanities Council; the winning essay appears in *North Carolina Literary Review*, Summer 2019. Her poems appear in *IthacaLit, Muse/A, CCLR, Rumble Fish Quarterly*, and *Stonecrop*. She blogs on Medium.com and at Howeverthink.com, and exists on various social media as oneofthejenns.

Mary Buchinger is the author of three collections of poetry: *e i n f ü h l u n g/in feeling* (2018), *Aerialist* (2015) and *Roomful of Sparrows* (2008). She is President of the New England Poetry Club and Professor of English and communication studies at MCPHS University in Boston. Her work has appeared in *AGNI, Diagram, Gargoyle, Nimrod, PANK, Salamander, Slice Magazine, The Massachusetts Review*, and elsewhere; her website is www.MaryBuchinger.com.

Kevin Burris lives in southern Illinois. His work has appeared in many literary journals, including *Poetry East, Atlanta Review, Southern Poetry Review,* and *The Bitter Oleander*. His first poetry collection, "The Happiest Day of My Life," was published in 2016 by FutureCycle Press.

Yasmin Mariam Kloth writes creative nonfiction and poetry. Her work has aired on NPR and appeared on npr.org. She co-translated a book of poetry by the French-Canadian author Mona Latif Ghattas called 'Sails For Exile,' and her work has appeared in *Gravel* and the *West Texas Literary Review*. She has work forthcoming in *The Tiny Journal, Willawaw Journal*, and *JuxtaProse*. She attended the Kenyon Review Writer's Workshop in July 2019 with Natalie Shapero. Yasmin lives in Cincinnati, OH with her husband and their young daughter.

Richard LeBlond is a retired biologist living in North Carolina. His essays and photographs have appeared in many U.S. and international journals, including *Montreal Review, Redux, Compose, Concis, Lowestoft Chronicle, Trampset*, and *Still Point Arts Quarterly*. His work has been nominated for "Best American Travel Writing" and "Best of the Net."

Cynthia McVay lives on a defunct farm in the Hudson Valley, where she writes, forages, and makes art. Cynthia's work has been/will be published in *DASH, The Ravens Perch, daCunha's Anthology 2, 2019 Orison Anthology, Ragazine* and *Eclectica*. Her work was winner, the 2018 Orison Anthology Award in Nonfiction; performed in the UK, as Editors' Choice winner, daCunha's 2017 Flash Nonfiction Competition; short-listed, Anton Chekov Contest New Flash Fiction Review; finalist, 2nd Annual — Sunshot Book Awards; Honorable Mention, Writer's Relief Peter K. Hixson Memorial Award: Short Stories; Honorable Mention, Glimmer Train Press's Very Short Fiction contest; finalist, Palooka Chapbook Contest; finalist, New Millenium Writings Muse Contest; finalist, freeze frame fiction and nonfiction finalist, Bridging the Gap Awards at the Slice Writer's Conference 2017.

Erin Schalk is a visual artist, writer, and educator who lives in the greater Los Angeles area. She graduated with her MFA in Studio from the School of the Art Institute of Chicago in 2017, and she has exhibited her art throughout the United States and in Japan. Today, Schalk teaches and is in charge of an arts education program which provides tactile art courses to blind and visually impaired students.

Aashika Suresh is a freelance writer from the Indian beach city of Chennai. She writes on days the world makes sense to her; and then again on days it doesn't. Aashika was placed among the top 30 poets in Wingword Poetry Competition 2017 and her work has appeared in Erbacce Press' chapbook, *Literary Yard, Wax Art and Poetry, Visual Verse,* and *Bones Journal,* among others. On most days, she seeks out good poetry, sunshine, coffee and puppies.

Katherine Szpekman writes poetry and memoir from her home in Collinsville, Connecticut. Her work has appeared in Red Eft Review, Sky Island Journal, and Muddy River Poetry Review, and is forthcoming in Hiram Poetry Review. She was awarded Honorable Mention in the Connecticut River Review Poetry Contest 2019.

Siamak Vossoughi is a writer living in Seattle. He has work published in *Glimmer Train, Missouri Review, Kenyon Review, West Branch*, and *The Rumpus*. His short story collection, *Better Than War*, received a 2014 Flannery O'Connor Award for Short Fiction.

Britnie Walston is a versatile artist, capturing energy through light, vibrant color, depth, and texture. The use of exaggerated brushstrokes and abstract color give her paintings life and voice. Her landscapes and abstract work consist of a variety of unconventional techniques to capture the elements portrayed. One of the most used techniques in her abstract paintings, is the method of mixing each individual color using acrylic paint, floetrol, silicone, and water. Together, they create "cell like" forms. Britnie also achieves different designs and textures using household objects such as strainers, straws, and frosting spatulas. She aims to depict the emotions of liberation ("set free") and freedom ("being free"). Her work as a whole, is inspired by nature and portrays the absence of human presence, bringing out the personality of nature itself, while providing the viewer the opportunity to escape and appreciate all the beauty that surrounds us. More of her work can be found at www.BN-WArt.com.

Chestnut Review

VOLUME 1 NUMBER 4 SPRING 2020

FOR STUBBORN ARTISTS

CONTENTS

Cover: Anni Wilson, "Naiad"
Linocut printed over stencil, 11" x 17", 2019

Introduction

Here we are at the last issue of Volume One. It has been a great ride so far, but how startling--yet thrilling--to mark a year of *Chestnut Review*. Consider this month's work:

Michael Steffen captures the beauty of not knowing in "Before Smartphones." **Leland Seese** describes the poignancy of a young girl's imagination in "What Is Swept Away." **Katherine Hoerth** shows the unintended virtue of misfortune in "Resurrection, Easter Morning." **Laura Perkins** paints a picture of friendship in "Howl." **Alan Feldman** reflects on transience in "April Snowfall." **Brittany Mishra** imagines the possibilities of environment in "Portrait in Gray." **Lois Marie Harrod** ponders the meaning of a not-so-simple word in "What's Token." **Alex Luft** examines language and life in "Terra Nulliparous." **Zebulon Huset** returns home, questioning, in his "In the dim garage I drunkenly pry again about the motivation behind his swastika tattoos."

We are pleased to feature art by **Michael Thompson** ("Skate Papers") and **Fabrice Poussin** ("Learning"); our beautiful cover ("Naiad") is by **Anni Wilson**.

Until summer, then. Keep creating, and being stubborn about it all.

James Rawlings

Before Smartphones

How long had you obsessed over the name of that band
that sang that song, *Stuck in the Middle With You?*
Religiously, you listened to WYSL's Top 40,
but the answer never came. Of course, you asked
your friends. Was it Ambrosia, King Harvest,
Mott the Hoople, Looking Glass? No one knew
for sure, but that was ok. Someday,
someone somewhere was bound to get it right.
You were just happy to be with your pals at Whitey's,
singing, getting wasted, talking drunken nonsense
about other times you got wasted
and all the random things you ever peed on—
police cars, garden gnomes, a piece of the
Berlin Wall in Vegas—anything, everything,
a whirling, tumbling gamble of language—*Dude,*
I can't believe you listen to Ambrosia. No one cared
if anything anyone said was correct. Point is,
you were together, swapping stories, memories,
arguing for hours, happily glossing over facts,
being vague. Conversation flowed freely back then.
If you wanted an opinion, you asked for it.
If you shouted your question to the air
after chasing four shots of Jäger
with a pitcher of Pabst while Honky Tonk Women

thumped from the jukebox, and some tanned,
bluesy beauty in tight jeans, tube top, tennis shoes,
reminding you of Mary Stuart Masterson
in *Some Kind of Wonderful*, separated herself
from her friends at the end of the bar, wandered over
to where you wobbled, back and forth, and whispered,
on tip-toe, into your ear—*Stealers Wheel*—you married her.

What Is Swept Away

I make coffee. She watches *Little Mermaid*.
No one else is up at ten-to-six. *It's low tide now*
I say. *Let's go to the beach and look*
for last night's treasure.

Pacific Ocean waves chant like monks at dawn,
Let there...be light. Fog and sunrise.
Tops of fir trees ranged like guardians
beyond the shrouded beachfront town
still sleeping.

Yesterday has been erased. The drama
will start over without fail, seagulls
hovered overhead, all-ages volleyball,
sand castles, salt-water taffy, lemonade.

She came to us two months ago, age 12,
a foster child — arrest of mother's boyfriend,
cell phone, pc hard drive seized.

This will be her first day
standing at the cusp of the wide open
ocean, something like a future.

I wonder if the people standing on this beach
500 years ago I say to her *saw exactly*
what we're seeing now. She's silent
longer than I think a 12-year-old can be.

She turns away and toes a clamshell
peeking out from gray-brown sodden sand.
She says *I never wonder anything.*

Resurrection, Easter Morning

It's Easter morning and the car won't start.
I'm witnessing this hopeless scene as April's
wind gusts bring my sable dress to life.
I'm the stubborn bud that doesn't open
as the miracle of spring sweeps over—
miles away at church as Jesus rises
from the dead, again. I sigh, resigned,
imagining the service now beginning
as it plays out in my wistful mind.
The plate gets sent around. My husband cusses,
rolls the sleeves up of his last good shirt,
leans beneath the hood and settles in
for an afternoon of finding out
what the hell went wrong with this, our bucket
of rust and sin. Together, we can fix
anything, he thinks. He's full of faith.
I'm full of doubt. He asks for tools, a wrench,
a ratchet, and a hammer that he'll use
for smashing our frustration into pieces.
I know the drill, this common ritual;
we've grown accustomed to it with a car

that's always on the fritz. The clock ticks on.
Now, we're missing it, I'm sure. The choir
must be belting out a halleluiah,
as the grackles all around us squawk.
Hipster Jesus rises from the tomb,
guitar in hand. I fiddle with the sparkplugs
praying beneath my tongue that this will work.
The preacher stands before the congregation,
minus us, declares the miracle
of resurrection once again, and though
I'm far away, I feel a certain stirring
in the heart. The car begins to cough
before the weary engine roars to life.

My husband laughs and takes me in his arms.
I wipe my grease-stained hands against his shirt
that mark it like stigmata of our morning,
breathe in the scent of him, his best cologne
mixed with sweat and gasoline and joy.
He says, *fuck church. It's crowded anyway*
on Easter. Let's get ice cream, love, instead.

Michael Thompson, "Skate Papers."
Collage, 2019

Howl

The cat we killed on accident. We were high from huffing spray paint out of a blue-splattered paper bag, my head scraped light and clean and floating somewhere to the left of me. Lola laughing, too loud—I slapped at her mouth, trying to create a seal. Smiley rose bitemarks ridged the skin along my fingers. I didn't feel it—or I did but the pain was something I sorted and put away for later. I caressed her cheek with my spitty palm. You can't tell me that anyone ever loved like we loved each other.

Lola wasn't her real name. She changed it from Lisa two years ago and we threatened anyone besides her parents who didn't use it. We couldn't do anything—we weren't fighters— but we liked to pretend, curled up on the pale purple carpet in Lola's bedroom. We flipped sticky magazine pages, our fingers dark from the cheap ink, and talked about the ways we would hurt if we could. "I would stab their eyes," Lola said. She was always about the eyes. I liked the idea of poison—a delicate slip of the wrist, no one knowing a thing.

We planned to get married to rich men and then murder them and take their millions. Those were the kind of women we wanted to be. "And then we'll move in together," I said, but Lola said no. "We'll have matching mansions next door. And a pool that connects. Then I can swim over to you when I'm feeling lonely." She mimed swimming on her carpet, bellyfirst, wiggling close to my ankle. Her smile had gone soft. We had taken pills from Lola's mother's medicine cabinet. We were always taking something, our days worthless if they couldn't be stretched or colored with some new beautiful thing to swallow.

"Why would you feel lonely if we're neighbors?"

"Because people are always lonely," she said, which is how I knew the drugs were taking a turn. Times like that the best thing to do was to curl up behind her and wrap my arms tight, let my breathing flow into hers. We fell asleep like that most sleepover nights, woke with sore muscles from clinging to each other like shipwreck victims.

We didn't mean to leave the front door open. We didn't see Marmalade dart out. We just wanted to feel the grass under our bare toes. It didn't work. The part of Wyoming where we lived was always in the middle of a drought, the grass stripped yellow and lifeless. Neither of our families had the money or desire to keep up neat lawns. Beneath our feet the yard was hard dirt and prickling stickers. Silent—even the bugs had moved on. We danced anyway. Lola and me, we're good about making the best of things.

On the weekends we went out with whoever would take us. Boys liked Lola better because she was prettier in that way they prefer, thin-boned and pale, but I let them put their hands all over me, so we were rarely alone. Jesse was nineteen and lived down the block from us in the trailer at the end, the one with the cropped-ear pitbull, Meatball, always barking his head off in the yard. Lola sat up front with him and I sat in the back with his fat cousin, Robert, utterly silent, possibly stupid. Crushed beneath our feet were grease-spotty pizza boxes from the

Dominos where Jesse worked weekday nights, though mostly he made his money selling weed he grew out of his closet. The weed was the main reason we liked him.

After an hour of driving around, the pot working in the back of my skull, I realized Robert had draped his thick arm around my shoulder. That's usually how it was—things were always in the middle of happening, their fingers somewhere on me. I didn't mind the weight. I always liked the feeling of being held down when I was high. I sat and met eyes with Lola in the rear-view mirror and pretended that I didn't notice Robert's fingers tapping along the exposed upper curve of my tit. You have to give something to get something, Lola says.

Jesse had a friend who had some mushrooms, or acid—"Something real strong." Of course we said yes.
"You girls got to be careful." Jesse held the cigarette in one hand, steering with his wrist. The other he draped over Lola's bare thigh. "We're okay, but you can't trust everybody. You get fucked up on everything and somebody's going to take advantage of you."

Boys were always telling on themselves. Lola goggled her eyes in the mirror. Her whites were blood-webbed, the pupils round black disks. My cheeks hurt from grinning—we both were, we looked insane. "It's okay," Lola said. "We're tough."

Jesse laughed. He squeezed Lola's thigh. His hand almost fit entirely around it. His fingers bit into her flesh but my girl didn't wince, didn't change her face at all. Robert's fingers slipped down farther, running along the underside of my bra lightly, pretending to ask permission. I wasn't yet high enough that I didn't care but I was getting there, my spine curved heavy against the seat.

"Real tough."

"We are," I said. "We've got super powers."

Invisibility or future vision—that wasn't for us. We wanted flash. We talked about laser eyes and super strength and poison saliva until Jesse got sick of it. "Shut the fuck up. Jesus. You girls are nuts."

That's always how it was—girls, the both of you. We were one thing, tied together—even our teachers thought so. Neither of us liked Jesse much but since Marmalade died, Lola's mother was depressed and her father was in one of his dark moods, and I didn't want to be home either. My mom worked late hours at a retail call center and delivered papers in the early morning. She was gone when I woke up. When she was home she was a lump of pulled blankets, words scribbled on the fridge. There was a new boyfriend, Patrick, who collected samurai swords and old guns. Lately he was home even when my mom wasn't, a pair of eyes watching from the couch, footsteps outside the bathroom door.

Lola and I talked about what we would do if he tried anything. "We'll use his swords," I said.

She agreed. "We'll start with his ears first." She mimed two sword strokes. "Snip, snip."

Cheyenne's streets died around ten, no cars or lights on anywhere. Sometimes Jesse or someone would drive us out to the railroads tracks near the east edge of town where there was hardly anything around. We wanted to do that tonight—to race around, arms out, heads tipped up towards the stars. "It will look so cool," Lola said, though we didn't know—we had never tried psychedelics. We'd taken things that made our muscles turn to soup, that made our hearts spasm, our stomachs cramp, that gave us nightmares—or worse, that did nothing. We wanted to see the stars fuzzed and colored strange. We were going to go where there was no backwash of light to block the sky. Last time we realized that you had to go farther than we thought to get away from all these people, to find a place open and empty of everything.

We waited in the car while Robert and Jesse went inside to get the stuff. We were on a side of town we hardly went to, north of the viaduct. Our street was all glass-bitten dirt and sloping trailer homes, but here everything was lush and green, the roads paved new. Lola crawled into the backseat with me and draped her legs over mine, our heads touching. Her thigh was already beginning to bruise where Jesse grabbed her. Lola had always bruised easily. My skin never showed a thing.

"Jesse's an asshole," she said.

"I know. We should rob him."

"Maybe the drugs will make him sleepy. Then you can seduce Robert. When he's out—bam!"

We always got so stupid on weed. We laughed quietly in the dark of the backseat. "No. I'll just knock him out, too. Then we'll steal their car and go to California." We had never robbed anyone. We had never really done anything wrong, other than to ourselves. We were all talk, but it was a thing we loved, the imagining—us as women with white coats and hoods fringed with fur, spiked nails painted red, cigarettes that we got other people to light for us. We were not college-bound. We knew the kind of lives we had ahead, the kind of lives all the girls in our neighborhood had—early pregnancies and diapers to change and boyfriends who beat us. Dull jobs scanning items at the checkout counter, a boss who liked to sniff our hair.

When Jesse and Robert got back, Lola crawled into the front again. It was part of the deal. I was so high that Robert had to shove me before I remembered to move over. Lola reached for the plastic baggy in Jesse's hand. He jerked it away. "Not here, for fuck's sake."

I leaned forward. "Come on. Please?" I batted my eyelashes, widening them, tilting my head, pouting. Sometimes I could put on an act, I could be funny. Sober and I was shy, I only spoke to Lola, but lit up with something and I didn't care what anyone thought.

Jesse allowed himself to grin, a little. Boys were easier if you could make them laugh—they felt safer, they looked you in the eyes.

"Puh-please?" Lola and I pasted our cheeks together, smiling, acting it up.

Jesse rolled his eyes. "Fine, fine, but just one."

Our hands darted for the bag. Of course we took more than one—we were always clawing for more than our share. Jesse tore the bag away and we put the shrooms in our mouths, chewing quickly. They tasted like the dirty wet end of a mop. Robert gave me a drink of his Mountain Dew to help get them down. His hand was around my waist now, I realized, palming the soft fat of my stomach.

"You did too much," Jesse said, peering in the bag. Lola and I caught eyes again, our grins flinty.

"There's enough left over," I said, but really, who cared?

We held a funeral, just Lola and me. She couldn't stand the sight of Marmalade's body, what the car had done to him, so it was my job to put him in the box. We sealed it up with his favorite fluffed pink blanket. We walked far out into the fields surrounding our homes, the knee-high grass causing Lola's allergies to act up, the tip of her nose glowing red, her sleeve snotty. We took turns holding up the barbed wire so the other could bellycrawl through to the other side. Above us the clouds were lazy and low-dipped, no shapes in them that we could find. I nicked my shoulder and by the time we got to a place Lola decided was good enough, I'd bled through my shirt. We were wincing, ducked-head things—mole people brought out to light, pale and hungover. When I touched my fingers to the skin of my temples I could feel my pulse beating.

We took turns digging the hole. The dry dirt was impossible, hard-packed with rocks, boulders. "Good enough," Lola decided when we'd dug barely a foot down. Her body was shaking, damp shadows under her armpits. The shovel had created and then torn open blisters on my palm and I had my hand in my mouth, sucking the rawest part. Marmalade's shoebox didn't quite fit, not straight. We placed him in and swept the dirt back over and pretended the jutting cardboard corner was another rock. We used the boulders we uncovered to weigh down the top. "That should keep the animals away," I said, though I figured it probably wouldn't, and I suspected then that we would never, ever come back out to this spot in case we found the earth opened, a scrap of blanket, a bone.

I waited for Lola to say some words. When we were kids, she found a baby bird that had fallen from its nest and we'd tried to raise it. Like we were kids in some Disney movie. It died overnight, of course. We buried it in her backyard. Lola wrote a poem which she buried with it. That was the way we were when we were alone together, the way Lola was unpeeled—soft, all the way down. But after a couple of minutes of staring, Lola said, "Let's go back. It's too fucking hot." So we left.

We went to my house, locking the bedroom door against Patrick, and lay on my narrow bed. I couldn't wait for her parents to get over Marmalade so we could go back to the way things were, back to Lola's house where the curtains were drawn back to let in the light, where we didn't have to creep, careful and soundless.

"Dad's moving past it. He's started talking about getting a dog. Now that's Marmalade's gone. He said we could get like a rottweiler or something."

"What about your mom?"

"She's still not talking to me," Lola said. "But she's always sad about something."

We drove into nothing, the darkness feeding us a few feet of road at a time. Jesse's headlights were dim, one flickering every time we hit a bump. I didn't recognize anything around me, but there wasn't anything to recognize—nothing but fields around us, the darkness shapeless and unbroken. Jesse played harsh music turned low while he talked about his dog, Meatball, and the things he was training him to do. I sat in the back gulping big, wet breaths. When I got too high my lungs always forgot their purpose. Lola knew how to calm me down—her fingernails along the back of my neck, ticklish-light. Scratchy-scratchy, we called it, but Jesse's arm was draped across the front and she couldn't get back to me.

Jesse's knee kept us on a waving line on the road while he dug into his pocket for the plastic bag. He shook half the contents into his mouth and then passed it back to Robert, who unwound his hand from wherever it was on me to take some for himself.

There were videos online, Jesse said, of pitbulls bow-legged and muscular. They leapt off walls. They dove through safety glass windows. If something was dangled in the air they would jump six feet to get it, to lock on, to shake until given the release word. The dogs ate nothing but raw hamburger and liver and slick white bones, still stringy with meat. They had no ears or tails. Their necks were spiked. Jesse and Robert were planning to take videos of Meatball as soon as they got a proper camera. "You can make so much money off YouTube," Jesse said. He was going to make his own dog food someday, his own channel. "Dogs like that, you can train them to do anything if you do it right."

"Where are we going?" Lola asked. I wished Robert would get his arm off me so I could breathe better. I missed home—not my dead house or Lola's, but the field around it where we wandered at night sometimes, too messed up on something to sleep but high enough not to feel afraid. We scratched our bare shins on weeds as we played explorers, we found garter snakes and wound them around our wrists like jewelry. We trilled our tongues to scare off any darting shapes and used the lights from our phones to guide us when we had gone too far. Someday we planned to disappear forever out there. "We'll become legends," Lola said. I said, "We'll eat bugs and learn to hunt with spears, and we'll kill anyone who tries to find us." Of course people would try. We dreamed of posters with our faces on them. We dreamed of being missed.

"It's all about dominance," Jesse was saying. "You have to let them know who's boss. They're like wolves—they need an alpha. When Meatball was a puppy, I would hold him down on his back whenever he was being a shit. I stared at his eyes. Dogs hate that, it freaks them out. He pissed himself. That's what dogs do to show submission."

When we were getting ready for tonight, Lola sprayed her pits with my mom's perfume and then twirled in the mirror. Earlier Lola's dad had come home and found the house a mess and her mom still in bed. He dragged her mom to the kitchen and made her watch while he pulled their cereal boxes down from the shelf one-by-one, carpeting the floor with flakes. "I just want to have fun tonight," Lola said. She added some of my mom's lipstick, a cheap, waxy red.

"You have to be tough or they won't respect you. It's kinder in the end—they love you afterwards," Jesse said. "It's like with kids. You don't want them to turn out spoiled or soft."

Lola's fingers moved around and around her mouth, as if she had something in the corner that she was trying to wipe away. "I don't think these mushrooms are doing shit." And: "Where are we going?"

When we fought, Lola was all sharp-knuckled jabs and barred teeth. She tucked her elbows close to her body like a boxer, eyes squinting over the ridge of her fists. My body was solid, shorter. I threw myself around; I didn't care how I landed. Unwilling to punch, I wrestled, pinning Lola to the ground while she scrabbled, jawing for my shoulder, my earlobe. It made us laugh, how bad we were at it. "Hit me," I said, and when I was numb I let her without raising my hands. I didn't flinch. Her knuckles a glancing brush along my cheeks. "Hold me. Grab me like you're trying to kill me." Lola would latch on from behind, her fingernails digging into my shoulders. A hug. We wanted to learn how to fight but it got us nowhere to practice on each other. Our hurts happened carelessly, on accident. We could never bring ourselves to aim and strike.

Jesse pulled off onto a narrow dirt road. He stopped in a field far from the highway. It was the kind of place where pieces of bodies turned up long after they were lost, scattered by coyotes and vultures. The wild yellow grass brushed our knees. The field was full of things that jumped, chirruped, a rattling somewhere. Robert wouldn't move from the car, eyeing the ground for snakes. Lola and I linked arms and ran in circles, stretching our legs. I felt high but not any kind of special high like I was expecting. Just stoned. The stars were out but we could hardly see them, navy clouds blocking their view. The only light was from Jesse's car. Yellow-tinged headlights illuminated a riot of dust and papery moths.

He found a coarse burgundy blanket in his trunk and spread it out on the grass. Lola and I stretched across it, flattening the grass beneath with our bodies. We stared up at the sky and I waited for anything at all to happen. My high was changing, smoothing out. I felt tired and I didn't want to, I wanted to run around, to stir up bugs. I wanted to have fun.

Jesse sat cross-legged at our feet, a cigarette jutting from the corner of his mouth. The glow from his phone lit up his face. Gnats, attracted to the light, swarmed his eyes and Jesse blew smoke through his teeth to scatter them. Insects flitted along my skin, tasting my sweat. Beside me, Lola was starting to shiver.

"Here, this is what I was talking about," Jesse said. A video played on his phone. The sound of a dog barking.

Neither of us looked. I didn't care about the videos and Lola was watching the sky, hands stretched towards it.

"Look," Jesse said, but no one looked.

"Where are we?" I asked.

Jesse grabbed Lola's ankle and shook. "Hey. Fucking pay attention. I'm talking to you."

Lola jerked out of his reach. She stood up and twirled in place, a wobbly ballerina. Jesse's eyes glittered in the light from his phone, pupils wide and watchful. He inhaled deep and let the smoke stream from his nostrils. Patchy stubble grew from his jaw. He was good-looking, but we knew things about him, Lola and me: We heard about the girlfriend with the fucked-up eye, the little brother sent to live with an aunt, the firecrackers thrown at kids and cats. It was part of the reason Marmalade wasn't allowed to be outside. That and the nearby road. Marmalade was too old; his eyesight was bad. He was too trusting. He would come if you called, tail high in the air, no matter who you were.

"How do you make money off of videos?" I asked. I didn't like the way he was watching Lola, the fix of his stare, unblinking.

"Ads. Clicks. The more you get, the more money you make. And then you develop products."

Lola stumbled. She fell to her hands and knees, giggling. I got up to help her stand. She used her teeth to pluck the stickers from her palms. She spit them out but badly, a mess of wet glistening on her chin. Her lipstick was almost entirely rubbed away, an animal red flare around her mouth.

"I taught my cat to roll over. When I got home from school he would run to this spot on the carpet and show me his belly. I taught him to go the rest of the way with this toy ribbon he liked. Then he would do it whenever I asked—long as I had treats. He knew his worth."

Jesse pinched off the lit end of his cigarette and tossed the filter away. He spit in the grass. His eyes were all pupil—an insectile black.

I watched the far-off highway, or at least where I thought it was. I wanted to count the seconds between cars, or the minutes, but for as long as I watched there was no one.

"Can I be in your videos?"

"I'm not putting your cat in my videos."

"My cat is dead," Lola said. She lifted her arms and then dropped them. "We buried him and everything. I meant me."

The ground felt soupy. I lifted my foot, one then the other, careful not to let my weight settle for too long. *Hey, something is starting to happen,* I wanted to say. My heart was too large. There wasn't enough room for it to kick blood through me, to all the places it needed to be.

"My videos are going to be about dogs. Didn't you hear me? Are you a fucking dog?"

"I don't know."

Lola, I tried to say. *Look.* The thought didn't connect to action. She was suddenly too far away, the path between us beginning to bend.

"Let's see." Jesse lifted his phone. The flashlight aimed at Lola. Her pupils reflected a milky light. "Be a good dog. Roll over."

Lola twisted in the air, then shook her head. Her mouth was pulling strangely in the corner. Smile-like.

"Hey," I said, or maybe I didn't. No one looked at me.

"I want treats. No treats, no tricks."

She laughed, the sound too high and sharp—glass shattering. I stretched my arm towards her. I needed to be near her, I needed her next to me. The ground wouldn't stop trying to swallow me and my arm had curved, the hair sticking up, an iridescent and lovely blur all along the edge of me.

"I gave you treats already. Now be good. Bark for me."

She thought it was a game until he stood up. He grabbed her arm. His hand was so large that his fingers overlapped her bicep. He squeezed. Her skin puffed between his fingers like raw dough.

"Bark," Jesse said.

Lola's mouth stretched. All of her teeth were showing, pink-smeared with lipstick. She tried to jerk out of Jesse's grasp but he didn't let go. "Stop," she said, and then she said it again. "Jesse, seriously. Stop. Let me go. Jesse."

The strain of his grip flexed the veins in his forearm. Lola's fingers dangled limp and bloodless. A line flickered between her pale, pale eyebrows. I watched it for too long, staring. Her eyes darted around until they found me.

"Come on. We're just fucking around. Just do it. Be a good dog."

Her fingers were swelling, plum-flushed. Lola tried to move again and made a sound deep in her throat, a sound she didn't want to make. She hated to cry. Even when we were alone she turned her face away, and I let her, petting her hair while she buried her face against the wall. After Marmalade's funeral I stroked her back while she tore her fingernails bloody with her teeth and made sounds I pretended not to hear, would never admit the relief in hearing.

"Jesse, come on," Robert said. I'd forgotten about him, unmoving from inside the car. This is all he would do—say something so later he could think himself the hero for trying.

Jesse lifted Lola's arm at an angle. I found myself moving across the sucking ground. My fingers light on his wrist. "Jesse, please. Please."

What I had to give away with that please. It was everything.

Jesse held his phone in his free hand. He aimed it at us and I wondered how we looked on screen—small against the blackness behind. Nothing anywhere. Just us, the two of us, looking back.

"Bark," Jesse said, and he lifted again and Lola inhaled and I knew he would break her arm. I would have to watch him break her arm. I would stand here, hands out, and hear the snap of it. Jesse's eyes, the flickering vein in his neck, his knuckles flashing white. I imagined my hands as claws, as fists, my eyes as lasers.

"I just want to have fun," Lola said. "I just miss my cat. I want to have fun."

"I'll do it," I said. Lola cut her eyes at me—a warning.

"Bark," Jesse said.

"I have to pee."

"Me too," I said. "We'll do it after."

Jesse relaxed his grip. He let go. Lola's hand dropped and swayed as if it wasn't a part of her.

"Fine," Jesse said. He kept the camera aimed towards us.

Lola and I walked away from the car. She took my hand. Her fingers were cold.

When there were enough yards between us, her hand pulled at mine and we ran. Jesse shouted after us but we didn't stop until we crested the top of a hill. We looked down at the shadow of him. I thought he would chase us but he stayed by the car and the light there, shouting. Lola tipped back her head and to the stars she yipped, barking awful and high and loud. After he gave up and drove away we would realize we were stranded, lost, but now we ran. Colors streamed from our fingertips. We laughed and ran and stretched our throats to the sky. We howled. We were wolves, wild things. I wanted to run forever. Our need, all that we wanted—you can't imagine.

A L A N   F E L D M A N

April Snowfall

I think it's because it's snowing—because
all around the house something beautiful is happening
silently, outside every window—that the world
feels graceful, even numinous. That's why we live here,
I think, where the world can contract to an intimate
stage set, a lacework of branches and snow

and falling flakes, that suggests a temporary beauty
so friendly to us, since we are temporary. It won't be
here tomorrow, and neither will we, we think,
and so its beauty is more flowerlike, as though the branches
are all laden with white blossoms, a snowfall
that is like a single song, fairly brief, surprising us

into tears. Before we were writing and painting, but now
it's snowing, and my wife is crying. Startling
how this patient silence shocks us into thinking
of transience. Not just the dead. But the living,
the frost gathering on their hair or beards. My wife
has been singing in her studio. She laughs about it

as she washes her brushes, her eyes reddened
and puffy. Some song her father used to play,
meant only to catch in people's ears and charm,

has become her prayer. Is she thinking of me,
here for a moment, like the snow? It's unfair to her
that the world is made to pass away, unlike a painting

made to archival standards. Here she puts the trees,
here the snow, that will not melt. Outside
the birds are silent, dumbstruck by the sudden change.

Fabrice Poussin, "Learning," 2019

BRITTANY MISHRA

Portrait in Gray

You have old eyes, your past
life framed black and white

packed away on tintypes,
but you've since colored yourself,

swung into the lake with full clothes,
seeped in its indigo blue.

You collect trout scales
to adorn your skin with rainbows,

and hide your memories
under the sturgeon's fin.

Fish gather as many lives as you do
dwelling at the bottom of the lake,

muscular and lean, they churn
futures into the red-brown deep

and you find in the water that time
is never the enemy, it is the quiet

pressure urging you to grow gills
and breathe.

A L E X   L U F T

Terra Nulliparous

The longer we stayed in Sydney, the more we wanted to have a child.

We were becoming solitary, nocturnal creatures that year. We woke early, around 4:30 a.m., so Abby could phone her co-workers back in Chicago. We spent our first hours in darkness. I would put a kettle on while my wife hoped our flimsy internet connection would hold. In June 2017 we'd moved into a tiny studio in the ritzy waterfront neighborhood of Kirribilli. We slept during odd hours, in a rented bed fitted between the couch and the patio door. The place was small enough I could reach into the refrigerator from anywhere inside the apartment, even the bathroom. We were alone on the far side of the world, Abby and I, but always within arm's length of one another.

On those mornings I would watch through the patio doors as a truck dropped dairy crates unguarded outside the shops of Kirribilli. Too early for milk thieves. I would change into a pair of shorts and Nikes and head out, minding the slick steps at the front of our building. I am a graceless runner, and so I was happy to get out before my lean Australian neighbors would see. I would lumber a quarter-mile to the stairs under the Sydney Harbour Bridge, where I'd huff my way upward.

The bridge path is just under a mile long, and if I timed it right, I would arrive on the southern side just as the sun began to rise. I often paused there, to catch my breath or pull at a cranky calf, but mostly to look out over the thick-forested headlands and the early ferries cutting through the harbor. I watched the first daylight splash up the walls of the Sydney Opera House and among downtown skyscrapers. On the days when no other joggers joined me, I felt so alone and so small, even while standing in the country's most populous city.

So maybe it was loneliness, or maybe it was the fact that Abby and I were usually within sight of that rented bed, but we thought daily about starting a family. We'd been married nearly five years, and we'd considered kids before. We were sidling up to our thirties. Abby had once told me her greatest fear about marrying me wasn't any of my myriad imperfections but instead the chance of infertility. Especially if it were hers. We knew people who'd struggled for years, through treatments and onerous adoptions. It was the kind of thing that could break a marriage.

To dispel the cramp in our Kirribilli studio, I would pull the patio door open as soon as the sun came up. In the dawn we listened to currawong calls and kookaburra laughs. The city woke around us. From inside our little place we could see flocks of children, *schoolies*, float by in ties and skirts and hats styled for a bygone century. And then it was less lonely.

Beauty, sometimes *Bewdy*, expresses approval. The *neural tube* is an invaluable cluster of cells that will one day become a baby's brain, spinal cord and backbone. For the people living in Sydney Park long before it was Sydney Park, a cormorant visiting the wetlands would have been called a *guwali*. The proper greeting is *how ya goin'?*

For the first time in my life, I began seriously to think about leaving America, if we got the chance to do so permanently. If my grandfather left his home country in search of a better life, I told Abby, why wouldn't I do the same? To us, Australia seemed – for a certain set of middle-class white people – a country that made good on its promise to give every citizen a *fair go*: nationalized healthcare, standard maternity leaves, four weeks of guaranteed annual holiday. It was easy for Abby and I to imagine our kids with Aussie accents, doffing their own school-uniform hats and swimming freestyle in their school's water carnival.

Our optimism, of course, was based on a painfully incomplete vision of the country. Aussies sometimes bristle at the cartoonish Australiana perpetuated by Paul Hogan and Steve Irwin and those *daggy* Outback commercials. Kangaroos, sharks, sun-bleached Hemsworths. Our friends back home asked after our encounters with crocodiles and deadly snakes (none happened) and the giant spiders (those did). But like any other place on earth, Australia is complicated and contested. These glosses obscure the country beneath.

On the lawn of Old Parliament House, in the capital city of Canberra, dozens of people live at the Aboriginal Tent Embassy. It is a semi-permanent camp of tents, mobile homes and RVs, established in 1972 as an ongoing demonstration urging government to return land to its indigenous owners. Signs and slogans abound. *White Invaders You Are Living on Stolen Land. Heritage Under Attack. Sovereignty.* The protestors' demands have gone unmet for nearly fifty years, but still Aboriginal activists live there, at a site of political struggle.

Abby and I were there, once, at the edge of the Embassy. Another stop on our tour of the capital. Between tents and canopies, people sat in circled lawn chairs, talking. A man in a blue-checked shirt knocked on the door to his neighbor's RV. It was midafternoon and quiet. Aboriginal flags hung limp on poles. The check-shirted man was finally admitted through the door. Nothing happened. Abby and I walked slowly and avoided staring.

A white Australian man and his two sons trailed us, taking pictures. We were voyeurs gawking at homes and lives, but the publicness of the Embassy is the entire point. Existence alone can be protest. The man behind us said nothing to his sons. Maybe he figured children make their own explanations.

Aussie kids enjoy *lollies*, of which milk bottles and snakes taste best. *Intrauterine growth restriction*, or IUGR, occurs when a baby fails to adequately grow in the womb. A dream is a *nangami* in the original language of Sydney.

That year, we walked. We didn't have a car, but we saw the region in a way that driving would have denied us. Abby and I would take after-dinner strolls along Lavender Bay and at least once a week, we'd set out for a longer hike, maybe as far as the Blue Mountains or as close as the Royal National Park.

Walking allowed me to explore, and it also reassured me of my body, in a way that is, I suppose, a privilege of being nondisabled. I enjoyed a sense I was made to walk, inherited from an ancestry of humans traversing incalculable miles. All I needed to do was ask my body to move me, and it would.

In that way, walking seemed like the opposite of our first attempts at pregnancy. About eight months into our Australian year, Abby was due to have her IUD removed, and so we started planning seriously. We knew we'd be returning to Chicago after a year, and Abby imagined stepping off the return flight with a growing belly.

Abby is a planner, a detail enthusiast, a master of spreadsheets. For her, pregnancy was a data project. Temperatures were measured. Calendars were drawn up with cycles, potential due dates and prospective maternity leaves. Planning, I knew, was a labor that women are expected to take up, even while I, the grinning husband, only had to supply the sperm.

But our approaches were as much about our personalities as our genders. Abby believes the world can be conquered or made better by the application of skill and intellect. Life can be managed, she figured, and so starting a life was no different. I, on the other hand, preferred fatalism. It would just happen for us, I insisted. Abby's body contained the reproductive structures, and we only had to ask them to move us along. Fertility was no different from walking.

One breezy morning we set out on the path that leads from Taronga Zoo to Balmoral Beach. The route wended along six kilometers of picturesque heads and lonely beaches, where water dragons sun on rock outcroppings or dart through the bush. While we walked, we talked about reproductive mechanics, especially how little we'd learned in school. Now we could calculate viability and list implantation signs. Abby was set to ovulate in the next week.

"I don't understand why it has to be so complicated," I said. We had just passed a massive web spun by a clutter of golden silk orb-weavers, one of the country's least lethal spiders. "Most people probably just let nature take its course."

"That's the story that gets passed along." Abby walked in front of me, checking the trail against a map we'd downloaded that morning. "After the kids grow up and you forget all about what it was really like."

We stopped at a split-off to make sure we were headed the right direction. The final section of the hike runs along Bungaree's Walkway, named for the first Australian-born man re-corded in print. A member of the Kurringai people, Bungaree's diplomatic skills so impressed explorer Matthew Flinders that the Englishman took him aboard to greet native people they encountered. Sometimes they let indigenous people believe the white sailors worked for Bungaree and not the other way around.

Bungaree's Walkway took us past a naval facility from which we could see our destination below. Unlike the tourists' Manly and Bondi, Balmoral is a neighborhood beach – at that time of day, it was trafficked mostly by locals *chucking a sickie* from work. Because Balmoral is sheltered in the harbor, its waters are calm enough for a relaxing swim. We descended the hill along a boardwalk weaving through teeming bushland, the promise of a dip in the saltwater not far off.

"So, we'll try this month," Abby said behind me, her steps clopping on the boards. "And if it doesn't work this month, we can try the next."

"It will work this month," I told her.

"How do you know?"

In Australia, to *root* is to fornicate and should not be used in reference to the footy club for which one *barracks*. In the Gadigal language, *putuwa* means to warm one's hands by the fire while gently squeezing a companion's fin-gers. If all goes, well the *zona pellucida* will degenerate five days after fertilization. To be *flat out* is to be exhausted.

Australia is a new nation built on old country. Aboriginal people have lived there in continuous cultures for more than 50,000 years, and for them, the white invasion led by Captain Cook is a short but still-unclosed chapter in a longer history.

Many white Aussies are proud to claim their ancestors among the 160,000 convicts shipped to the continent until 1868, but they are sometimes less apt to acknowledge decades in which churches and governments forcibly moved children from Aboriginal communities into white homes. It wasn't until 2008 that the Prime Minister Kevin Rudd acknowledged the Stolen Generations and the fractured families left behind.

The same year as Rudd's "Apology," Parliament adopted a *welcome to country* for its official opening. In a welcome to country ritual, an elder of the local language group will speak and might perform music, dancing or smoke rituals. In New South Wales, where Sydney is located, a welcome to country is required for all state-run events. Where a local elder isn't present, speakers substitute an *acknowledgement of country*, in which they pay their respects to the site's *traditional owners* past and present. I came to expect this acknowledgement at the start of any public event – a footy match at the Sydney Cricket Ground, an academic conference, or a museum tour.

Neither the welcome nor acknowledgement are universally embraced. For one, it's difficult to reconcile the Eurocentric language of ownership with the more nuanced relation that many Aboriginal people hold with the land and water. Some versions of the acknowledgement refer to the first Australians as *custodians*, but one can see how this language, too is flawed, as if the caretaking relationship between country and people is one-way, rather than mutual. But perhaps most trenchantly, the acknowledgement and the welcome are symbolic acts without any meaningful justice attached. Acknowledgement does not entail legal ownership or economic value. These are imperfect symbols in an imperfect nation.

A few months into my time at Macquarie University, I was set to give a guest lecture, and I'd seen a few classes open with an acknowledgement of country. There had already been a formal version at the opening of the term, and so it wasn't necessarily expected for every week's presenter to give one. I debated whether I should. On the one hand, it seemed important for a people in positions of power (even relatively little power, like mine as a graduate student) to signal solidarity with the practice. On the other hand, I didn't understand all the dimensions of the act, and worried I would be engaging in sheer tokenism. Even now, writing this, I worry the attempt that speaking *about* Aboriginal people entails speaking *for*, and it would be better I find some white American male silence.

It would have been easy enough to find a standard script online to recognize the Wattamattagal clan of the Darug Nation, but I forewent the acknowledgement that day. I was, I told myself, no child of Australia. Theirs was not my history to undo.

Putting in the hard yards means you're doing difficult work. From the word government, *gubba* is Aboriginal slang for whites. *Teratogens* are the things that can delay, deform or disrupt a human in utero. Everyone likes to say *no worries*.

I arrived home from teaching one night, after having jogged down the steps of the Milford's Point train station and past sidewalk diners at the Fitzroy Street restaurants. Teaching always left me enervated, but I always hurried home, anything to return to the private little world of the studio apartment. Abby had set out a salad for dinner and was watching *Who Do You Think You Are?*, a program in which Australians trace their ancestries through historical records, inevitably finding family trauma interlaced with wreckage. She kissed me hello and paused the show long enough for me to grouse about my students and a two-minute delay on the train.

I sloughed my satchel into the corner opposite the bed, where I kept my books stacked haphazardly on a pair of end tables. A little brown bag sat atop the books. I looked at Abby, who smiled and waited. Inside the bag was a tiny T-shirt, a smiling bear imprinted on it. And with it, a postcard, in Abby's handwriting: "You were right. You usually are."

She gave me the details of a positive pregnancy test. She'd already taken a follow-up, just to make sure. It had taken all her self-control, she admitted, not to tell me earlier, but she didn't want to get my hopes up for no reason.

We spent the rest of the night talking and planning: when the baby would come, how we would arrange prenatal care in Sydney, whether we should immediately rule out all names starting with A (alliterative families being one of my chief phobias). I told Abby I hoped the kid would somehow adopt an accent in utero.

A woman doesn't get pregnant in Sydney; she *falls* pregnant. *Primip* is shorthand for *primipara*, a woman during her first pregnancy. It can also refer to a woman with just one child. A *multip* is a woman who has given birth more than once. A woman who has given birth once but is pregnant with her second is also a *primip*, not yet a *multip*. It would be reductive to think of *mob*, which often refers to a tribal group or extended network, as interchangeable for *family* among Aboriginal Australians.

In the early 1970s, Eddie Mabo worked as a gardener at James Cook University. He'd been born on Murray Island, situated in the Torres Strait, before moving to Townsville, which had once been known as the Thuringowa area. The popular version of Mabo's story is this: a couple of history professors were eating lunch when Mabo—known to friends as Koiki—stopped for a chat. They started talking about his ancestral home, the island that he would have called Mer. It was a lush place with a volcanic center. It was home to eight tribes, including Mabo's ancestors. He often thought about returning to his land there, he told the historians.

His land? They had to break it to him. The island didn't belong to him. It belonged to the Crown. It had been discovered by the British.

No, Mabo insisted. His people had a system of inheritance that had lasted more than 2,000 years before whites arrived. He was a rightful heir.

But when the settlers had come, they didn't or couldn't see the people living on the island—couldn't see them as people, as legitimate owners. Like the Australian mainland, Mabo's friends might have told him, the island was claimed under the colonial legal principle of *terra nullius*, or nobody's land. International law stipulated that if territory wasn't populated (or, perhaps, insufficiently used or built upon), the colonizing power could freely claim it. And thus terra nullius was deployed in legalizing invasion and genocide by denying that such things could have even taken place.

In the 1970s, Mabo and other Aboriginal activists brought lawsuits against the Australian government, challenging ownership based on the misapplication of terra nullius. White Australians were asked to acknowledge their land had, generations ago, relied on their ancestors pretending Aboriginal and islander communities hadn't existed. In some cases, these claimants denied the same indigenous people that had helped settlers survive in the rugged bushland.

Mabo and four of his Mer-born compatriots hoped to legally establish their ownership of Murray Island, arguing against the legitimacy of terra nullius. For ten years, their case was heard before the Queensland Supreme Court and the High Court of Australia. Mabo's was a test case for the nation's so-called "history wars," a litany of public debates about whether Australia was built on a relatively peaceful collaboration between colonizers and indigenous communities, or whether the Australian story was actually one of dispossession and exploitation.

Mabo died in 1992, five months before the court ruled to overturn all terra nullius claims. The next year, Parliament passed the Native Title Act to formally acknowledge indigenous land claims, allowing some latitude for Aboriginal and Torres Strait Islander communities to decide how to use their ancestral grounds and waters. About 15 percent of Australian land is now recognized as belonging to its traditional owners, typically managed through more than 600 Land Use Agreements, under which control is still a matter of negotiation with the Australian government.

Three years after Mabo's death, following a celebration of the court case that would come to bear his name, vandals spray-painted swastikas and slurs on his tombstone. They stole a bronze stature erected in Mabo's likeness – another desperate attempt to deny his existence.

For contemporary Aboriginal people, the word *deadly* connotes excellence. *Gravida*, from the Latin word meaning "heavy," refers to pregnancies no matter the outcome. Young Australians, especially, use the shorter *devo* to mean "devastated." *Nulliparous* refers to a woman who has never given birth, *gravida* notwithstanding.

I never saw it – the blood. I don't know whether it trickled or clotted or just flowed. I didn't ask. I remember Abby walking through the door of the bathroom, only a few feet from the couch where I sat. I wanted to see, maybe. I wanted to go and gaze into the water and see what was there or not there, but it had already been flushed away. Maybe if I had seen it I would be able to say, to think, what *it* was.

We did what anyone of our generation does. We took to the internet, first to deny the worst, then to deconstruct it. Medical knowledge about early pregnancy is incomplete, largely because it is impossible to observe some of the initial germination. Pregnancy is something of a black box; we know what goes in and what comes out. It is nearly impossible to say, in any individual case, exactly what mix of chemical or organic arrangement was inhospitable for life to develop.

If Abby and I hadn't watched so closely for that first pregnancy, we might have never known it was there. It might have passed without us thinking twice. Surely this happens to countless women, countless times.

In any case, ours seemed – not just then, but soon after – such a minor tragedy. It wasn't a pregnancy we'd agonized over for months, and it wasn't the loss of a child. We hadn't struggled, or seen fertility doctors, or undergone treatments. Less than a footnote to a footnote's footnote in the history of human tragedy. Barely enough for an essay, even.

And yet, in the days after I scrambled for explanation. I resorted to – maybe I romanticized – a roughly translated version of Aboriginal epistemology, one that posits a non-hierarchical structure for the world. In this line of thinking, there are complex natural systems, but even humans must perform their role the same way sea kelp or a wombat or even a rock might. People don't own the earth but in some sense *are* the land and water and animals. There is no great difference between people and not-people because all things flow into one another.

And so, I wanted to believe, whatever had been there – bundle of cells or protein-formations or insignificant biological matter – it *had been there*, person or not. That might be enough to mourn, if only I could know for sure.

If you're far from buildings and power lines and streets, you're *in the woop-woop*. As many as 75 percent of miscarriages can be attributed to *chemical pregnancy*, which medical providers describe as a random occurrence, during which chromosomal abnormalities prevent full implantation. *Wellama* means to return or come back.

There once was a place called Yerroulbine, but by the time we stepped foot on the notch of bushland jutting southward into Sydney Harbour, it was Ball's Head Reserve. Abby and I had ridden the train northward to Waverton station on a Sunday afternoon, with snacks and bottled water bouncing in my pack as we trekked through a middle-class neighborhood of federation-style homes.

At the north end of the reserve, we followed a path to a defunct coal loader, where a tunnel ran through the massive concrete structure. When we stood at one end, the rectangular hallway subverted our sense of scale. It looked like the other side might have been thirty feet away, or three yards, or maybe a third of a mile. The sun, bright as it was outside, could not penetrate the middle stretches. Water dripped and pooled. For almost a hundred years this had been the site of frenzied industry, men stacking and pulling and carting coal. Before that, it had been pristine bushland in the Wollstonecraft Estate, and before that, home to the Cammeraygal people. Now it lay quiet. We walked through.

In the middle of the tunnel, in its darkest spot, rock surrounded us totally. Buried us. We stopped for a moment there. Abby didn't say anything, and neither did I. I looked back the way we came. It might have been farther away than the other side. I couldn't say. We kept on.

We walked past organic gardens and the Coal Loader Centre for Sustainability, built recently in an effort to undo the environmental damage of the previous century. Past that, gum trees gave shelter to flying foxes, some of the megabats we often saw circling overhead in the Sydney twilight. The trails at Ball's Head also led us past caves Sydneysiders had made into homes during the Great Depression. The squatters carved out shelves and bunks and rooms, so they might sit cross-legged around a fire, looking out over the slow roll of the harbor. The paths led, too, past sites of Aboriginal art, burial spots and middens. Loss and renewal in an indelible cross-hatch through the earth.

At the tip of Ball's Head, just off the path, we scrambled down the rocks to a cliff-face high enough from the waves the spray couldn't touch us. We were supposed to talk about going home. I was due to book our return flight to the states, where we faced the discomfiting prospect of resuming the life we'd had before. We would have some hard choices about which things to pack into our luggage and which to leave behind.

I opened the backpack and pulled out our water bottles and a couple of apples. The rock was damp beneath us, but the place was sunny and quiet and unforgivably beautiful. The city rose sparkling on the south side of the harbor, ferries and party boats punctuating the waves between us and downtown.

We could find another apartment back in Chicago, we figured, and buy new furniture. I told Abby I was lukewarm about the prospects of returning to my doctoral program. We didn't talk about trying again. Not yet.

"Should we tell people?"

"People never talk about it," Abby said. "Especially when it happens so early. I don't even know what to say."

"Should we use the m-word?"

She shook her head, sipped at her water bottle. "No. That's not right."

It wasn't, of course. A miscarriage requires a fetus, and our – whatever it was – didn't make it that far. What you call a thing matters. The language calls it into being. We could call it a loss, maybe, and let people understand what that meant.

We didn't know then that it wouldn't be our first loss, or that, after we'd become disillusioned and decided to take a break for a while, the losses would stop.

We had seen a dozen other hikers around Ball's Head that day, but on the rock overlooking the water, we felt alone. The city could be like that.

The air off Sydney Harbour is salty and thin and carries music, the calls of cockatoos and waves against the rocks of Barangaroo. A city of gleaming towers and dim-sum houses and pie shops and beachfront cafes throbbed along the edge of the water, and still the magic loneliness of the place was undeniable. It was possible to feel totally at the cusp of life, isolated enough to touch the boundaries of everything. To think about everything that had been there and everything yet to come.

"I threw away the card," I told Abby, "the one you gave me that night."

She nodded. "You weren't wrong. You just didn't know."

In the dim garage I drunkenly pry again about the motivation behind his swastika tattoos

I passed a bottle of Jack Daniels with neighborhood kids
fifteen years after I'd left—on the coattails of turning 18—

kids I used to play freeze tag with at the bus stop
or who my mom used to watch for Day Care.

I'd missed their formative years, the slow slide of
the neighborhood into an entropic suburban Sons of Anarchy

parody where the heroin & brass knuckles left bruises
& tracks & drew blood that looked pretty damn real.

I just remember playing hide & seek with these kids—
watching their LA Lights trail off through the side yard.

Ryan, that little hockey-obsessed runt was over 250 now
& eager to tell me about how during his last time inside

all he had to do was take off his shirt in the yard
& his tats did the talking. Multiple large swastikas.

I'd missed a significant span of his life. Sure, he was shoplifting
cards by the time I'd left—a typical middleschool kid—

but I wasn't holier than thou. He would always be
part bowl-haircut goalie stopping my slapshot tennis balls.

But somewhere he found a strange path, & though
there may have been more racism than I recognized at the time,

we were always more of a Workers of the World unite,
pull-your-own-weight, we're-all-equal sort of zone

as far as I'd known. Even our Lutheran Church seemed,
to me— a blue-haired skate punk—more of a passive voice

that judged you to a point but then shrugged & moved on—
I think you may go to hell, but you do you I guess—

was the threat of hellfire filtered through Minnesota-Nice.
So I wanted to know why white supremacy. So I asked.

I was genuinely interested, but my much-nearer sober wife—
San Diego native, alien in the sub-zero weather but not to prejudice—

refereed from the sidelines, eyes wide because she imagined
a quick-to-violence party in Klantee, Santee's fun nickname

all-too-familiar to her teenage years. But these were my people,
my lost sheep, I could lead them back into the fold of non-assholes.

I was about that level of drunk. Apparently I was an idol there.
I'd escaped—made it to the coast like a wagoneer, lived the skate-dream

which was interesting—I'd forgotten the dream hadn't always
included being rich enough to not work. We'd all worked.

It's who we were. We were hardworking Scandinavian stock
solid in the cold, mittenless mostly but more pragmatic than proud.

We understood toil & we loved stories—each eager to add
our own tall tale to the bonfire. Ryan never really got my questions,

but also didn't think I was fucking with him & break the bottle
over my head & gnash the smashed glass stem in my eye.

Really, I wasn't fucking with him—I wanted him to have a drunken
epiphanic moment & change his ways, because, I don't know

it would be like my own little indie movie. Jessica & I held hands
as we walked in the twilight to the third garage or basement party

in the night of liquor-hopping my still-underage sister had networked,
ending with basement video games & more beer in the quiet backyard

of my older brother's best friend's house, not for that tie but
because my younger brother & sister were tight with his brother—

the suburban web so thickly interwoven you could string it
between two evergreen branches, lay supine & inhale the piney air.

We used to roam the streets on green maple leaf evenings
all night at miles range. We cut through yards, hopped fences,

we caught the tiniest toads you've ever seen at the library pond
behind Richard's house, brother of my brother's once-best man.

Outside, the uneven patio held puddles just at that perfect icing-over
where you could tap it & leave it intact or tap & snap it.

We breathed mist & listened to the sound of cold-resistant birds
already preempting the sun with their incessantly upbeat peeps.

What's Token

Black, of course. For light I left behind.
And the white librarian's chary hello

because of my hand, my skin,
flat accent sliding south. This voucher—

as a paper poppy, a pink ribbon,
stands for unsuffered suffering.

The ice cubes melting in the arctic
for the coming hurricane,

the lock on the bedroom door
which sometimes kept you out

and maybe the ragged kale left by the deer,
the half tomato rejected by the slug.

Certainly, last year's book left in vacation's lodge
and the little heart I wore around my neck

until the Penrose Trail, the watch
you gave me when the baby was born,

all we couldn't afford, keepsake
stolen. Children diminish

into forgotten toys—
ragged dolls and three-wheeled trucks—

and everything stands for something—
the t-shirt frayed at the neck, the sock

thinning at the heel, the heel worn
down from so much walking.

Some nights even the fading star seems
a coin for a life I could have lived

and again I am left anxious at the lavatory door,
the toll booth, the subway gate wondering

if what I have in my hand
will allow me to enter one more time.

CONTRIBUTORS

Alan Feldman's poetry has appeared in *The Atlantic, The New Yorker, The Nation, Poetry, The Kenyon Review, The Southern Review, Ploughshares, Iowa Review, Threepenny Review, Virginia Quarterly Review, Yale Review,* and others. His full-length collection of poems, *The Happy Genius* (New York: Sun, 1978) won the 1979 Elliston Book Award. *A Sail to Great Island* (University of Wisconsin Press) was awarded the 2004 Felix Pollak Prize in Poetry. Another collection, *Immortality*, published by the University of Wisconsin Press in 2015, was awarded the 2016 Massachusetts Book Award for Poetry. His latest collection, which received the Four Lakes Prize from the University of Wisconsin Press, is *The Golden Coin* (2018). The National Endowment for the Arts and the Massachusetts Artists Foundation have awarded him fellowships in poetry. He lives in Framingham, MA and, in the summer, in Wellfleet, MA, and currently offers free, drop-in poetry workshops in those towns. He is married to Nan Hass Feldman, an artist.

Lois Marie Harrod's 17th collection, *Woman,* was published by Blue Lyra in February 2020. Her *Nightmares of the Minor Poet* appeared in June 2016 from Five Oaks; her chapbook *And She Took the Heart* appeared in January 2016; *Fragments from the Biography of Nemesis* (Cherry Grove Press) and the chapbook *How Marlene Mae Longs for Truth* (Dancing Girl Press) appeared in 2013. A Dodge poet, she is published in literary journals and online ezines from *American Poetry Review* to *Zone 3*. She teaches at the Evergreen Forum in Princeton and at The College of New Jersey. Links to her online work: www.loismarieharrod.org

Katherine Hoerth is an Assistant Professor of English and Modern Languages at Lamar University and serves as Editor-in-Chief of Lamar University Literary Press. Her work has been published in journals such as *Georgia Review, Atticus*, and *Valparaiso Review*, among others. Her poetry collection, *Goddess Wears Cowboy Boots*, won the Helen C. Smith Award for the best book of poetry from the Texas Institute of Letters. In 2018, she was inducted into the Texas Institute of Letters. She lives in southeast Texas.

Zebulon Huset is a writer and photographer living in San Diego. His writing has recently appeared in *The Southern Review, Louisville Review, Meridian, North American Review, Fjords Review, Portland Review, Texas Review* and *Fence,* among others. He publishes a writing prompt blog (Notebooking Daily) and his flash fiction submission guide was featured at The Review Review.

Alex Luft's work has appeared in *Yemassee, Midwestern Gothic* and other magazines. He reads prose for *Quarterly West* and teaches writing in Chicago.

Brittany Mishra helps make airplane engines for a living and writes poetry and fiction as her passion. She's lived on both coasts of the US, but now she lives in Washington state, near the Puget Sound, with her husband. Brittany's poetry can be found in Shabda Press' *Nuclear Impact Anthology* and the online journals *Voice Catcher, Sky Island*, and *The Write Launch*.

Laura Perkins lives in Cheyenne, Wyoming. Her work has appeared or is upcoming in *Cutbank, Cagibi, The Mighty Line*, and *Sky Island Journal*.

Fabrice Poussin teaches French and English at Shorter University. Author of novels and poetry, his work has appeared in *Kestrel, Symposium, The Chimes*, and many other magazines. His photography has been published in *The Front Porch Review*, the *San Pedro River Review* as well as other publications.

Leland Seese's poems appear in *Juked, Rust+Stars, The South Carolina Review, The MacGuffin,* and many other journals. His debut chapbook, "Wherever This All Ends," was published in March (Kelsay Books). He and his wife live in Seattle with a revolving cast of foster, adopted, and bio children.

Michael Steffen is a graduate of the MFA writing program at Vermont College and the author of three poetry collections: "No Good at Sea" (Legible Press, 2002), "Heart Murmur" (Bordighera Press, 2009) and "Bad Behavior" (Brick Road Poetry Press, 2013). Individual poems have appeared in *Poetry, Poet Lore, Potomac Review, Rhino*, and other journals. New work will appear soon in *Chiron Review, Thimble, Lily Poetry Review, Street Light Press* and *The American Journal of Poetry.*

Michael Thompson is a third year illustration student at The Ontario College of Art and Design University. He works in a hybrid of analogue and digital, focusing on either physical paper cutting or digital paper cutting.

Anni Wilson is a print-maker working in a combination of linocuts and stencils. Her work is set in the universe of the Industrial Revolution, a period whose themes resonate with those of our own: class divides, gender inequalities, capitalistic greed, and the alienating effects of technology. Her recent work has appeared or is forthcoming in *Folio, The Emerson Review,* and *Reed Magazine.*